S0-BDA-276

RACING
TACTICS

Also by Manfred Curry

YACHT RACING

Ed Cox, at the tiller, and Ed Muhlfeld, on the foredeck of Shields 22, leading the fleet as they prepare to jibe around a reaching mark during a Shields Class Regatta on Long Island Sound. (Photo: Fusanori Nakajima)

RACING TACTICS

by Manfred Curry

Completely revised
by Edward J. Cox
and Edward D. Muhlfeld

Charles Scribner's Sons, New York

Copyright © 1973 Charles Scribner's Sons
Copyright 1949 Manfred Curry

This book published simultaneously in the
United States of America and in Canada—
Copyright under the Berne Convention

All rights reserved. No part of this book
may be reproduced in any form without the
permission of Charles Scribner's Sons.

1 3 5 7 9 11 13 15 17 19   V|C   20 18 16 14 12 10 8 6 4 2

Printed in the United States of America
Library of Congress Catalog Card Number 73-5171
SBN 684-10095-9 (cloth)

To the memory of Dr. Manfred Curry

Contents

Acknowledgments

We wish to thank the following individuals for their assistance:

From *Yacht Racing*, Knowles Pittman; Bruce Kirby, Editor; Don Graul, Managing Editor.

From *Boating* Magazine, Sydney Rodgers, Publisher and "Monk" Farnham, Editor.

From *Flying* Magazine, Bud Loader, Creative Director.

From *Photography* Magazine, Shin Tora.

Jerry Schneider, Assistant Secretary of Ziff-Davis Publishing Company.

William S. Cox, Steve Colgate, and Jim Linville for technical assistance.

Harry Anderson of the North American Yacht Racing Union for his cooperation in obtaining the NAYRU Rules.

Our devoted wives Mary Jane Cox and Diane Muhlfeld without whose patience and typing capabilities we would not have a book.

EDWARD J. COX
EDWARD D. MUHLFELD

Preface

Dr. Manfred Curry, one of the world's most famous yachtsmen, learned sailing from his father, Dr. Charles Emerson
Curry. He won his first race at the age of twelve in the presence of King Ludwig at the Ammersee, his summer home in
Bavaria. Questioned by the King as to his success, Curry shyly
explained that at the last moment a skipper lacking one in
crew asked if he would like to be the replacement, to which
he enthusiastically agreed.

Shortly after the start their position appeared hopeless,
and the crew losing all further interest offered the helm temporarily to the young boy. Within a very brief period the
boat's position improved to such an extent that the skipper
asked Curry to return the helm. He refused and, with the
technical knowledge and experience gained while sailing with
his father, was able to maneuver the boat from last place to
first.

During his life, where sailing was only one of many avoca-
tions in which he excelled (for Curry was in fact a doctor of
medicine and scientist, and wrote numerous books on the subject), he won more than twelve hundred first prizes, twenty-

four hundred second, and countless others, a record not improved upon this day. At the age of eighteen he wrote his famous book, *Yacht Racing*, later referred to as the "Bible of Sailing," followed by *Racing Tactics*. Both were published by Scribners in the United States, and later translated into seven languages and sold throughout Europe. In 1949 Dr. Curry revised the books, and since his death in 1953, twenty years later, the rules of racing have in many instances changed, thereby requiring this revision.

With the sincere hope to all yachtsmen—whether their intentions are to become professionals in the field, or simply to relax and enjoy the great beauty and pleasure of sailing—as the wife of the late Dr. Manfred Curry, who lived in greater part his enthusiasm and love for sailing, I wish you the best of luck in your endeavors.

MAUD CURRY

RACING
TACTICS

Introduction

How To Use This Book

Although many books have been written about yacht racing in all its many and various aspects, very few have used the "question and answer" format. Most educators agree that the question and answer technique is a most effective teaching tool, since it lends itself easily to repetition: the key to any learning process. Dr. Manfred Curry in 1932 recognized the effectiveness of this technique and used it as the basis for his book on racing rules and tactics.

Dr. Curry was well in advance of his time, for today we see and hear much about "programmed instruction" and other similar learning techniques, all based on the simple question and answer method.

In this revision, we have retained the question and answer format, for we feel it is still one of the most effective teaching methods. As in Dr. Curry's original book, all questions and supporting illustrations will be found on left-hand pages, and all answers with their illustrations on right-hand pages.

This permits students to ask themselves questions and

read the answers at their own pace. If you don't know the correct answer to a question, that answer is readily available on the opposite page. If you *do* know the correct answer to a question: proceed immediately to the next question, and so forth, until you get to a question you can't readily answer. Every student will have his own rate of progress and each student will progress as fast as he is capable of progressing, or as fast as he wants to. The basic elements of programmed instruction are (a) immediate and clear answers to questions; (b) repetition of answers until they become known; and (c) the ability of a student to go quickly through those questions he already knows and to spend whatever time is necessary on the questions he cannot readily answer.

The Rules

Many people find yacht racing rules difficult to learn and remember; that's why they are an ideal subject for a programmed instruction technique.

All of the yacht racing rules, as adopted by the North American Yacht Racing Union (NAYRU), have been included in this book. All of the rules' changes which became effective on May 1, 1973 have been incorporated. You will find the NAYRU rules printed in the first section of this book; a grey tint band on the outer page edges will set this section off from the rest of the book for easy reference. Do not be concerned with the apparent bulk of the rules: only two sections out of the six (which comprise the total rules) have a significant bearing on this book. They are Parts I, "Definitions," and IV, "Sailing Rules When Yachts Meet."

How To Learn the Rules

Newcomers to sailboat racing should read parts I and IV of the racing rules carefully, not trying to memorize them, but trying to understand and become familiar with them. It may seem like a tedious job, but if taken in small doses and

4

learned carefully the rules are not particularly difficult to understand. The questions in Chapter 2 ("Racing Rules") have been organized in the same procedural order as the rules themselves. Constant reference is made to rule number and page number, so that a reader, in studying the answers, can easily refer to the rules' section of the book and reread the applicable rule in its entirety.

At first glance the reader may find Part IV of the rules confusing. So here's a summary of the basic, or most important, rules that may help to put them in better perspective:

Section B: "Opposite Tack Rule"
   Rule 36 (Port/Starboard Situations)

Section C: "Same Tack Rules"
   Rule 37 (Windward, Leeward Yachts)
         (Clear Ahead, Clear Astern)
         (Overlaps)
   Rule 38 (Luffing After Starting)
   Rule 39 (Sailing Below a Proper Course on
           Free Legs of the Course)
   Rule 40 (Luffing Before Starting)

Section D: "Changing Tack Rules"
   Rule 41 (Tacking or Jibing)

Section E: "Rules of Exception" *
   Rule 42 (Rounding or Passing Marks)
   Rule 43 (Hailing for Room to Tack)
   Rule 44 (Yachts Returning to Start After
           Premature Start)
   Rule 45 (Yachts Re-rounding After
           Touching a Mark)

* These Rules override those in Sections B, C, and D if there is a conflict.

The thirty-five questions and answers which comprise Chapter 1 of this book are probably the most important for the serious skipper. These questions should be read carefully and the answers thoroughly studied. The authors urge all readers to use the programmed learning method outlined above, since this technique will assure a basic understanding of the racing rules. After the thirty-five questions are fully understood, you will be much better prepared to move into the chapters on racing tactics.

The Rules as a Basis for Tactics

Practically every tactical situation involves a rule; knowledge of the appropriate rule will be most important to a skipper faced with a sudden tactical decision. He must instinctively know which rule(s) apply, what his rights are, and how he should properly maneuver. Only a thorough and complete knowledge of the rules will enable a skipper to freely employ the tactics discussed in this book.

Yacht Racing: A Year-Round Activity

However, while racing rules and tactics are perhaps the most important part of yacht racing, there are many other factors that can affect the outcome of a sailboat race.

In the fall of the year, as your boat is hauled for winter storage, you must:

> —inspect all standing and running rigging;
> —make all necessary major repairs, such as mast work, rebuilding of winches, etc.;
> —prepare the bottom: sanding, smoothing, fairing;
> —order new sails and other equipment.

In the spring, before your boat is launched, you've got a lot more work to do. First: final smoothing of the bottom and painting with appropriate anti-fouling or racing-finish paint; second: final inspection of all rigging, all mast fittings, all winches and mechanical equipment; third: replacement of all necessary running rigging; and, finally: relocation (if necessary) of sheet leads, cleats, etc.

Once your boat has been launched, but before the first race day, set the mast so it stands perfectly straight in the boat; then adjust it fore and aft to give it a neutral helm, or perhaps a slight weather helm.* Then sail with your crew; train them in their respective duties.

The Day of the Race

On race day, before leaving shore, make sure you get as much information as you can about tide and current; study the race circular; listen to a weather forecast.

Before the starting signal, a skipper intent on winning will sail hard on the wind and set his sails properly in accordance with that particular day's wind and wave conditions. This means proper adjustment of outhaul, downhaul, backstay, cunningham,** jib sheet leads, jib halyard tension, etc. He will set up his mainsheet and jibsheet, and position his crew according to their weight so that his boat seems to be sailing at optimum speed.

Strategy vs. Tactics

At this time, a good skipper will formulate his basic strategy for the windward leg. Do not confuse strategy with racing tactics; the latter don't come into play until the race is about to start.

Racing strategy concerns the location of a yacht on the race course, and the determination of what series of maneuvers will bring it to the next mark fastest. Strategy involves an evaluation of the effects of tidal currents, shorelines and other obstructions, probable or possible wind shifts based either on weather forecasts or "local knowledge," the effects of either

* Weather helm: the tendency of a yacht to turn head-to-wind when the helm is left unattended.

** *Cunningham,* or *"cunningham hole":* an adjustment that controls the depth and location of the draft in a mainsail.

stronger or lighter breezes over different areas of the race course, the effect of wave action on a yacht given a particular course and a known wind condition, etc.

Racing tactics, on the other hand, generally means boat-to-boat maneuvering, or the effect of one boat on another. And since the subject of racing by its very nature implies proximity of yachts to one another, the racing rules become very important. Rules and tactics are very closely related and, along with strategy, form the basic elements of sailboat racing.

Strategy is, more or less, your game plan, carefully thought out in accordance with today's conditions, and constantly updated throughout the race as new information is acquired.

Whenever possible, the observant skipper will watch preceding classes after their start to see what strategy seems to be paying off. A good skipper will also measure the length of the starting line (converted into sailing time), and will have two stop watches aboard in case one fails. He will decide whether or not one end of the starting line is favored over the other by measuring the angle of the wind to the line. The good skipper will take all of these things into consideration in deciding upon his overall strategy.

Quite often, the type of cloud buildup, or the direction the clouds are moving, is a forecast of future wind conditions. Generally speaking, where clouds are building up (or where you can see a thunderstorm or thundershower forming) there's stronger wind. If you can, sail toward the clouds.

But the whole subject of weather is a book in itself, and varies widely according to area and season.

Having formulated your strategic plan, and with countdown to the starting signal about to begin, racing tactics come into play.

Another way of looking at it, and briefly stated: strategy is you vs. the race course, while tactics is you vs. the competition.

The Scope of This Book

As Manfred Curry wrote, and as we can attest, yacht racing is a complex, complicated sport. It is an all-encompassing hobby that can keep a serious yachtsman busy throughout the year.

Dr. Curry, in his original treatise, concentrated on tactics and on a complete understanding of the racing rules. These, he felt, and we agree, are the basic and most important areas of the sport. This book, therefore, concerns itself only with yacht-racing rules and tactics. No attempt is made, other than in the Introduction—and here in the most superficial manner —to cover yacht preparation, tuning, weather interpretation, or racing strategy.

To become a winning skipper, however, one *must* study these other areas, and many texts are available that treat them in far greater detail than they've been discussed here.

As a skipper gains confidence in each of these areas, his total knowledge and competence will greatly broaden, as—in terms of yacht racing—all are closely related. The best tactician will win no race in which his basic strategy is wrong or his boat is improperly tuned. A foul bottom or a skipper's failure to notice a wind shift ahead will negate total recall of every racing rule. All of these elements work together to produce a winner.

The better a racing skipper sails, the closer he will be to the top sailors in his class or fleet. Racing against this tougher competition reaps its own reward, for thus will a skipper learn many additional fine points of yacht racing through observation. Each step gets him closer to the time when he will cross the finish line with all of his competition behind him.

And make no mistake: as confounding as the task of preparing for, sailing, and winning a yacht race may be, the boom of the first-place cannon is the sweet music to a skipper's ears that makes the whole thing worthwhile.

Good sailing and good luck.

EDWARD D. MUHLFELD *and* EDWARD J. COX

Comments
from Dr. Curry's
Original Introduction

"How does it happen that always the same helmsmen are successful—and what are the requisites for their success?" This question is often put me and always embarrasses me to a certain degree; either I am, at the moment, not quite sure myself just wherein the success lies or I realize the question cannot be answered satisfactorily, or at least not in a few words.

In order to demonstrate the manifoldness of yacht racing,* one part of which, racing tactics, is treated in this volume, a general exposé, analyzing the psychology of a yachtsman and the requisites for success in this sport, is outlined in this introduction.

The superior qualities and abilities that, when combined, lead to success in regattas are partly intellectual and partly based on innate traits of character such as feeling. Both are influenced by experience. The various qualifications or requi-

---

* The technique of sailing and the application of fundamental tactical maneuvers to racing, as also the scientific investigation of sails, etc., are treated in the author's volume entitled *Yacht Racing—The Aerodynamics of Sails and Racing Tactics,* published by Charles Scribner's Sons, 1948.

sites for success in racing may be grouped according to their importance, as follows:

1. Tactical ability—racing tactics.
2. Knowledge of wind-technique.
3. Technical sailing ability.
4. Quickness: (a) of thought;
   (b) of action.

Of next importance are:

Knowledge of the weather, endurance, concentration, self-confidence, knowledge of human nature, courage, foresight, precaution, etc.

Regatta Tactics

or the various methods of combat: It is astonishing how superficially this comparatively new but decisive science is treated by many yachtsmen and with what prejudices it is regarded especially by those of the older generation. It can no longer be denied that a regatta consists chiefly of combat—attack and defense—and that the old method of simply sailing over the racing course without any regard to one's competitors no longer leads to victory. One is forced either to defend oneself against competitors astern, or to attack those in the lead. In our present highly developed science of yacht racing it seems ridiculous to attempt attacks to the weather, which under normal conditions are doomed to failure, or to give up a good lead simply from lack of tactical knowledge. A good tactician is bound to win every duel and will always prove his ability in a race, even when he is not in the lead, by being able to overtake many of his competitors before the finish. He who can sail his boat through a large field—from the last place into the leading group—is a master of tactics.

Until only a few years ago tactics, with the exception of maneuvers for the weather berth and blanketing, were practically unknown in yacht racing. In the meantime, they have been developed to a most complicated science with its many details and variations. As many as two hundred kinds of duels and fifty or more different buoy-maneuvers may be enumerated. The leeward berth has superseded the weather berth in many situations, perhaps in the majority; these ideas of modern tactics, which were promulgated in my book *Yacht Racing*, were pronounced as absurd and ridiculed even by experienced yachtsmen upon the book's appearance some years ago. Who would have then admitted that there are many tactical situations which can be saved and won only by voluntarily retarding the speed of one's boat, by letting her sails flap or by some other means? Or that the number of tacks made on a beat to windward—upon approaching a weather mark—might be decisive.

. . .

In general, it is not justifiable to speak of bad luck in racing; for why should good skippers always have good luck? There are, of course, moments, when the wind may be very tricky, showing no indications whatever beforehand for such behavior; in fact, there are tactical moments that are decided by luck; however, there is only one such moment to my knowledge for which the helmsman may not be held responsible. It is the following: We are leading at the mark and the ensuing leg is a beat to windward; we hold our two nearest competitors, boats 1 and 2, in our blanketing zone; boats 3, 4 and 5, which are following in the wake of the leading group, go about onto the other tack upon reaching the mark. The field is, therefore, diverging in two groups at an angle of about 90°. As we cannot be in both groups, what then, if the tack chosen by the group in the rear proves to be the more favorable one—due to veering of the wind or some other cause? Although we may be leading or even increasing our lead in our own group, we may, upon having split tacks with the other group, find ourselves beaten by all three boats of that group. This misfortune can befall any helmsman, especially in waters with which he is not acquainted, and still he certainly cannot

12

be blamed for lack of foresight or pronounced an inefficient tactician.

The Knowledge of Wind Technique

is the second qualification in our list. If tactics alone were decisive, yacht racing would soon be a tedious sport. The combination of tactics with wind technique, however, leads to innumerable situations and possible variations, the successful solution of which requires rather intellectual, logical thought in the application of the tactics than a mechanical memorizing of tactics proper. For example: How are the tactics toward one's various competitors to be modified, when the wind heads one off, veers toward the quarter or changes its direction entirely? These are considerations, to which the helmsman must constantly direct his closest attention and thoughts. The form—mode of application—of many a tactical measure varies with both type of boat and strength of wind. When one's boat begins to plane, tactics must undergo a certain change. Tactics and wind technique often oppose each other. One may frequently have to desist from carrying out a promising aggressive measure or to abandon a tactically safe defensive position, in order to gain a greater wind technical advantage. For instance: by going about,—with the intention of catching a favorable gust of wind. But it can happen that the too zealous skipper, like the gambler in Monte Carlo with the desire to "win still more," on his speculations with the wind loses the whole of his good lead. This is a characteristic peculiar chiefly to skippers who are not quite sure of their tactics and being in doubt trust rather to chance than to their own ability as tacticians. It is surely very tempting to run after a promising gust, even if one has to let one's competitor escape in doing so; but the risk taken is generally quite out of proportion to the advantage gained, and I am inclined to the opinion that a leading boat in a good defensive position should not seek to better her position through wind technical maneuvers, but should direct her attention only to tactical

13

measures and principles, that is, to her competitors. The helmsman who has had the sad experience of repeatedly sacrificing a good lead by a tack apparently justified by wind technique will not again be so easily lead astray by this risky maneuver.

Technical Sailing Ability

This is synonymous with the most favorable position and handling of the sails and their sheets, proper trim of boat, correct tending of centerboard, etc. It is the science of making the boat travel at maximum speed and is, to a great extent, a matter of experience. One notes under what conditions the boat attains her highest speed—how close her sails are trimmed,* how far over she may be heeled to advantage, to what depth the centerboard and rudder blade may be lowered, etc. A good scientific education and a certain technical and aerodynamical knowledge will be found to be of great assistance in solving these various problems. Which jib should be set? Under what conditions does the funnel effect appear? How should the spinnaker be set with regard to the mainsail? These are questions that cannot always be answered even after careful observations on a series of trial spins. We know, for instance, that with the wind abeam a boat will travel fastest, when her sheets are properly tended—the jib sheet in such a manner that the relative position of the jib to the mainsail produces the effective funnel-effect; this effect is established, when the air current in lee of the mainsail is not broken off.—Moreover, we recognize the great importance of not allowing a centerboard boat to heel in a strong wind. Only a clear understanding of the parallelogram of forces and of the resistance of the water will enable one to appreciate the value of such factors. The experienced helmsman on a small racing

* In 1973, sail trim is the most important of these factors, particularly in one-design classes, where all the sails are theoretically identical—built by the same sailmaker, cut from the same bolt of cloth, and often drawn for by lot among the various members of a racing class.—Eds.

14

craft will carefully observe the direction and strength of every gust on the water long before it reaches his boat, instructing his crew to be ready to lean out to windward before the gust strikes the sails, and he will ease off the mainsheet as soon as his boat shows the least tendency to heel. The experienced skipper is aware of the fact that there are very few yachtsmen who can tend the mainsheet of a small boat properly in a strong wind. I may state from my own experience that I recall only two yachtsmen who have tended the mainsheet on my boat to my full satisfaction. As a dancer should move his shoulders but little when dancing, similarly a boat should be so balanced, by joint tending of the sheets and shifting of the crew, that in the strongest gusts she will heel only appreciably, that is, her mast will be only slightly inclined.

An old technical error, especially of the more experienced skippers, is that of pressing their boats in light airs. A prominent skipper of small boats once observed quite to the point: "If the wind is the soul of the boat, her life is manifested best by letting her run full and by." One invariably forgets that a boat should only be pressed in sailing to windward when it is absolutely necessary owing to some urgent tactical maneuver, of which there are, however, very few. In several races I have requested my crew to keep reminding me to "let her run and give her a good full." Although I was fully convinced of the truth of this old proverb, I did not succeed in overcoming this contagious fault until only a few years ago. The experienced yachtsman will surely confirm my view-point that at least 90 per cent of all skippers suffer from this sympathetic disease through mutual infection.

The situation, however, is quite different in the case of a strong wind. One has to let one's boat work up into the wind, sometimes with her sails partly flapping. My technique in beating to windward in smooth water consists in hauling the sheets in taut, in having the crew well up and leaning out to windward, and in letting the boat run higher and higher on the wind—without the least regard to the racing pennant—until she is sailing quite upright. The best method of parrying a gust from the quarter is to luff before it strikes the boat; in other words, on the windward leg one conserves all surplus driving force or energy at once by luffing rather than by the heeling of the boat.

The correct handling of the tiller is also to be included under the heading "technical sailing ability." The tiller of a yacht should be moved less—slower and more carefully—than that of a small boat, which must be steered by greater—quicker and often sudden—movements of the tiller; the real secret of steering either yacht or centerboard boat lies, however, in putting her on her fastest possible course with minimum loss of speed while obtaining this object.

. . .

Quickness of Thought and of Action

To think quickly is one thing, to act quickly another. There are helmsmen who think quickly but seem quite unable to put their thoughts into action owing to a certain timidity, uncertainty or lack of self-confidence. There are others, who think slowly or not at all, but act quickly on the advice of others, or if, by chance, an idea suddenly occurs to them. It is just as important for the sportsman as it is for the surgeon to be able to think and to act quickly. Without being aware of it, the subconscious mind is capable of carrying out three or four trains of thought simultaneously. A tennis player who excels at the net will surely be a good yachtsman, at least one who is quick in acting.

. . .

We next proceed to the transmission of thought into action. The speed therein attainable is a matter of practice. It was always one of my chief ambitions in racing to be the quickest in all maneuvers. In order that my crew may attain the greatest speed in the execution of their maneuvers, I always begin to rush them when setting the sails and in making

the boat clear for the race. It is only by this means that I succeed in getting them into proper shape for the race—to be
quick enough. I exhort them to work "faster," "still faster,"
"not yet fast enough," that they may become accustomed to
the speed I require of them later—during the race.

Quick action must be preceded by quick thinking. The
competitor must be taken by surprise in all tactical measures,
so that, before he has time to consider the correct defensive
move, it is too late for him to carry it out. With equal tactical
ability the quicker one will win the game. Just a fraction of a
second faster in thought and action than your competitor suf-
fices to confuse him and make him nervous. You must be the
first to have your spinnaker up and drawing, should the wind
suddenly change or veer in the right direction. Such promptness is always a sure sign of quick decision on the part of the
helmsman.

The quickness of thought and action is outstanding at the
start. The science of a successful start consists in tactical ability, quick thinking and acting, careful observation and, last
but not least, experience. . . .

.   .   .

We finally come to the attributes for a successful sailor
that are of minor importance: knowledge of the weather, endurance, concentration, self-confidence, knowledge of human
nature, courage, foresight, precaution, etc. A knowledge of
weather conditions is naturally of great advantage to the
sailor; it enables him to forecast bad weather, a thunderstorm,
etc. and to be prepared for it when it finally breaks loose, to
decide in advance whether he should reef, which jib he
should set—the small or the larger one—or for example to
judge when and under what conditions strong air currents, indicated in the upper layers of the atmosphere by swift flying
clouds, will reach the lower layers and finally the surface of
the water. These are questions that may decide the outcome
of a race.

Endurance, both physical and mental, including concen-

17

tration of thought and action, is also a most essential attribute for the racing man. It is no small matter and not to everyone's taste, to have to concentrate one's thoughts for hours, from the start to the finish of a race sailed in light airs or a calm, and to refrain from partaking in any refreshments till the race is finished. I must confess that I myself never found time for refreshments of any kind during an important race.

The remaining attributes of minor importance, self confidence, courage, foresight, precaution, knowledge of human nature, etc., are to be regarded more as qualities of character —innate properties—than as abilities or efficiencies, the latter being acquired chiefly by practice and experience. There is perhaps no vocation in which character manifests itself more strongly than in sport. . . .

Self-Confidence: This apparently insignificant attribute plays, though imperceptibly, an important role in every race. "I will win and I shall win—I cannot lose," should be the leading motive of every skipper; "Our helmsman must win— he cannot be beaten," that of his crew. When a prize fighter, upon entering the ring, remarks: "I shall beat him," such a remark is to be construed not as a sign of arrogant conceit but rather of the absolutely essential self-confidence. I have often noticed what a terrible effect it has on the helmsman, when his crew alarm him during a race by saying that "the other boats are drawing near," instead of encouraging him by saying, "They are again falling astern," or "They will not pass us." The crew must have implicit confidence in their skipper and, even if they do not, they should at least forebear from showing it. I remember when I once sailed as a member of the crew with a very poor skipper. Had I shown the least inclination to rob him of his last bit of self-confidence, the race would have been lost—from the very start; but by assuring him "fine"—"excellent"—"good move," etc. I encouraged him and surely accomplished more. On the other hand, I despise a yachtsman who complains about his crew to others; if they make mistakes, it is not their fault but his, he picked them out as his crew and should have given them an opportunity to train, or should have trained them himself before the race to his own satisfaction. I think that most yachtsmen will agree with me that implicit faith or self-confidence is often the secret of success.

Knowledge of Human Nature is also a desirable attribute in yacht racing. Every skipper should observe, in fact, make a study of his competitors, so that he may become thoroughly acquainted with their various traits and indirectly their mode of racing. This is most essential in tennis, boxing, etc. It is good to know, for instance, that a competitor is of a sullen nature—he may smile, but is, nevertheless, capable of luffing suddenly and unawares; another may be only pretending to luff and will protest on the first opportunity offered; a third competitor we know to be fair—a good sportsman—he might, or might not be acquainted with the various maneuvers and tricks and counter maneuvers; another can be easily fooled by a feigned move or attack, etc.

Also the correct relation of courage to precaution is essential in tactics and very often decides a race. It is unwise, for example, if one has a good lead to make unnecessary maneuvers in a blow, especially upon approaching the finish—often merely for the purpose of "showing off." All such superfluous maneuvers reveal bad taste and are designed chiefly for the uninitiated, not for the true sportsman. The setting of the spinnaker under such conditions may cost one the victory and perhaps the mast. On the other hand, the considerations of a boat in the rear should be quite the reverse—in conformity with the saying "rather capsize than not make every attempt to win"; here the spinnaker and all auxiliary sails should be set even if it is blowing half a gale.

A weakness common to some skippers is that they lose all confidence and presence of mind the moment they lose the lead. The greatest mistake they can then make is to stop fighting for the lead and begin to speculate wildly. This invariably leads to disaster. If your competitors astern overtake you and you lose the lead, you should not get discouraged; you should not sail with lack of energy; you should, coolly, realizing your situation, act as if the race had just begun. Such a critical situation is, in fact, much more interesting and satisfactory to the tactician than a lead of a mile or so, a race won with little exertion and without the necessity of resorting to tactical measures.

Finally, upon investigating the mentality or temperament of helmsmen from a more general point of view, in order to form a concrete conception of this class of sportsmen, we must discriminate between three distinct groups: Those who have had much experience in racing and strive to profit by it,—those who have an inborn talent for racing,—and those who possess both; in other words,—the ambitious skippers,—the talented ones—and the always successful ones. Similarly in tennis there are three groups: those who have attained proficiency from long and careful training, who, so to say, return every ball; their training has made them sure but not necessarily speedy and enables them to play a careful, but rather tedious game—void of especial interest to the spectators.—Others play a fast and exciting game, of the greatest interest even to the initiated, but they cannot always be relied upon; they lose as often as they win, and victory depends to a great degree upon whether they are in "form" or happen to have a so-called "good day."—The third group comprises the first class players, the champions; they play a game worthy of tennis, interesting and exciting in every respect, a consistent, so-called "heady," absolutely sure and very fast game.——The corresponding class of yachtsmen, the champions excel in avoiding mistakes, in acting quickly and, above all, in carrying out all their maneuvers consciously and logically from beginning to end. Their premeditation is the secret of their success. They avoid speculating—trying doubtful maneuvers;

20

they do not wait for their fate, they determine it themselves; and, last but not least, if defeated, they always know why they have lost.

Manfred Curry

1

1973

The Yacht Racing Rules Including Team Racing Rules

OF THE

International Yacht Racing Union

AS ADOPTED BY THE

North American Yacht Racing Union

For the convenience of the reader, vertical lines have been added to the left-hand margins, in Part IV of these rules to indicate *significant* changes which were adopted by NAYRU on May 1, 1973.*

NOTE: In translating and interpreting these rules, it shall be understood that the word "shall" is mandatory, and the words "can" and "may" are permissive.

* Rules printed courtesy of NAYRU.

Right of way when not subject to the racing rules

The rules of Part IV do not apply in any way to a vessel which is neither intending to race nor racing; such vessel shall be treated in accordance with the International Regulations for Preventing Collisions at Sea or Government Right-of-Way Rules applicable in the area concerned.

See Appendix 8.

1973 CHANGES

As in 1969, the 1973 rules include a good many small changes for consistence and better understanding.

Rules 22.3, 67, 74.3 and Appendix 3 are new. So also, but of different application, are Appendices 4 and 5.

Without implying that other changes need not be examined, attention is called to rules 32, 34, 35, 40, 42.1(*a*)(ii), 52.2, 73.2(*b*), the team racing rules and Appendix 6.

For ready comparison most changes, even when only the number of the rule, are indicated by a vertical line in the left margin.

FOREWORD

Effective May 1, 1973, the North American Yacht Racing Union has adopted as its official racing rules the racing rules, including the team racing rules, of the International Yacht Racing Union. No changes are contemplated until 1977.

The I.Y.R.U. rules permit certain changes and additions by National Authorities. In order to assist North American yachtsmen when racing abroad and visiting yachtsmen when racing here, rules so changed or added have been identified by placing a star (☆) in the margin beside them.

Of the twenty-three rules listed in this paragraph the following eight rules have been changed by the N.A.Y.R.U. and have been starred (☆) except rule 72.4 which has been deleted. The I.Y.R.U. text of these rules is given in Appendix 7.

8.1, 18, 24, 25.2, 28, 72.4, 77, 78.

The following fifteen rules have not been changed by the N.A.Y.R.U. other than to be printed without the phrase "unless otherwise prescribed (or if so prescribed) by the national authority" or words to that effect:

1.4, 2(*j*), 3.1, 3.2(*b*)(xvi), 4.1, 4.2, 4.4(*a*), 10, 23, 24, 52.2, 54.2, 56, 57, 62.

All the above twenty-three rules should be checked for differences when sailing under the jurisdiction of another national authority.

A graduated penalty in Appendix 3 and a prescription to rule 68.4(*a*) in Appendix 6 have been added and starred (☆).

The following three starred (☆) rules have been added by the N.A.Y.R.U. on matters not covered by I.Y.R.U. rules:

51.6, 53.2, 79.

North American yachtsmen will find the above information of significance to them only when racing under the jurisdiction of another national authority. For racing under the jurisdiction of the N.A.Y.R.U. the starred (☆) rules are to be treated like any other rules.

TABLE OF CONTENTS

PART I

DEFINITIONS

When a term defined in Part 1 is used in its defined sense it is printed in **bold** *type. All definitions and italicized notes rank as rules.*

Racing—A yacht is **racing** from her preparatory signal until she has either **finished** and cleared the finishing line and finishing **marks** or retired, or until the race has been **cancelled, postponed** or **abandoned,** except that in match or team races, the sailing instructions may prescribe that a yacht is **racing** from any specified time before the preparatory signal.

Starting—A yacht **starts** when, after fulfilling her penalty obligations, if any, under rule 51.1(*c*), Sailing the Course, and after her starting signal, any part of her hull, crew or equipment first crosses the starting line in the direction of the course to the first **mark.**

Finishing—A yacht **finishes** when any part of her hull, or of her crew or equipment in normal position, crosses the finishing line from the direction of the course from the last **mark,** after fulfilling her penalty obligations, if any, under rule 52.2, Touching a Mark.

Luffing—Altering course towards the wind until head to wind.

Tacking—A yacht is **tacking** from the moment she is beyond head to wind until she has **borne away,** if beating to windward, to a **close-hauled** course, if not beating to windward, to the course on which her mainsail has filled.

Bearing Away—Altering course away from the wind until a yacht begins to **jibe.**

Jibing—A yacht begins to **jibe** at the moment when, with the wind aft, the foot of her mainsail crosses her center line and completes the **jibe** when the mainsail has filled on the other **tack.**

On a Tack—A yacht is **on a tack** except when she is **tacking** or **jibing.** A yacht is on the **tack** (**starboard** or **port**) corresponding to her **windward** side.

Close-hauled—A yacht is **close-hauled** when sailing by the wind as close as she can lie with advantage in working to windward.

Clear Astern and **Clear Ahead; Overlap**—A yacht is **clear astern** of another when her hull and equipment in normal position are abaft an imaginary line projected abeam from the aftermost point of the other's hull and equipment in normal position. The other yacht is **clear ahead.** The yachts **overlap** if neither is **clear astern;** or if, although one is **clear astern,** an intervening yacht **overlaps** both of them. The terms **clear astern, clear ahead** and **overlap** apply to yachts on opposite **tacks** only when they are subject to rule 42, Rounding or Passing Marks and Obstructions.

Leeward and **Windward**—The **leeward** side of a yacht is that on which she is, or, if **luffing** head to wind, was, carrying her mainsail. The opposite is the **windward** side.

When neither of two yachts on the same **tack** is **clear astern,** the one on the **leeward** side of the other is the **leeward yacht.** The other is the **windward yacht.**

Proper course—A **proper course** is any course which a yacht might sail after the starting signal, in the absence of the other yacht or yachts affected, to **finish** as quickly as possible. The course sailed before **luffing** or **bearing away** is presumably, but not necessarily, that yacht's **proper course.** There is no **proper course** before the starting signal.

Mark—A **mark** is any object specified in the sailing instructions which a yacht must round or pass on a required side.

Every ordinary part of a **mark** ranks as part of it, including a flag, flagpole, boom or hoisted boat, but excluding ground tackle and any object either accidentally or temporarily attached to the **mark.**

Obstruction—An **obstruction** is any object, including craft under way, large enough to require a yacht, if not less than one overall length away from it, to make a substantial alteration of course to pass on one side or the other, or any object which can be passed on one side only, including a buoy when the yacht in question cannot safely pass between it and the shoal or object which it marks.

Cancellation—A **cancelled** race is one which the race committee decides will not be sailed thereafter.

Postponement—A **postponed** race is one which is not started at its scheduled time and which can be sailed at any time the race committee may decide.

Abandonment—An **abandoned** race is one which the race committee declares void at any time after the starting signal, and which can be re-sailed at its discretion.

PART II

MANAGEMENT OF RACES
Authority and Duties of Race Committee

The rules of Part II deal with the duties and responsibilities of the Race Committee in conducting a race, the meaning of signals made by it and of other actions taken by it.

1—General Authority of Race Committee and Jury or Judges

1. All races shall be arranged, conducted and judged by a Race Committee under the direction of the sponsoring organization, except as may be provided under rule 1.2. The Race Committee may delegate the conduct of a race, the hearing and deciding of protests or any other of its responsibilities to one or more sub-committees which, if appointed, will hereinafter be included in the term "Race Committee" wherever it is used.

2. For a special regatta or series, the sponsoring organization may provide for a Jury or Judges to hear and decide protests and to have supervision over the conduct of the races, in which case the Race Committee shall be subject to the direction of the Jury or Judges to the extent provided by the sponsoring organization.

3. All yachts entered or **racing** shall be subject to the direction and control of the Race Committee, but it shall be the sole responsibility of each yacht to decide whether or not to **start** or to continue to **race**.

4. The Race Committee may reject any entry without stating the reason.

However, at all world and continental championships, no entry within established quotas shall be rejected without first obtaining the

29

approval of the I.Y.R.U. or the duly authorized international class association.

5. The Race Committee shall be governed by these rules, by the prescriptions of its National Authority, by the sailing instructions, by approved class rules (but it may refuse to recognize any class rule which conflicts with these rules) and, when applicable, by the international team racing rules, and shall decide all questions in accordance therewith.

2—Notice of Race

The notice of a race or regatta shall contain the following information:—

(*a*) That the race or races will be sailed under the rules of the I.Y.R.U., the prescriptions of the national authority and the rules of each class concerned.

(*b*) The date and place of the regatta and the time of the start of the first race and, if possible, succeeding races.

(*c*) The class or classes for which races will be given.

The notice shall also cover such of the following matters as may be appropriate:—

(*d*) Any special instructions, subject to rule 3.1, which may vary or add to these rules or class rules.

(*e*) Any restrictions or conditions regarding entries and numbers of starters or competitors.

(*f*) The address to which entries shall be sent, the date on which they close, the amount of entrance fees, if any, and any other entry requirements.

(*g*) Particulars and number of prizes.

(*h*) Time and place for receiving sailing instructions.

(*i*) Scoring system.

(*j*) That for the purpose of determining the result of a race which is one of a series of races in a competition, decisions of protests shall not be subject to appeal if it is essential to establish the results promptly.

3—The Sailing Instructions

1. **Status**—These rules shall be supplemented by written sailing instructions which shall rank as rules and may alter a rule by specific reference to it, but except in accordance with rule 3.2(*b*)(ii) they shall not alter Parts I and IV of these rules; provided, however, that this restriction shall not preclude the right of developing and testing proposed rule changes in local regattas.

2. **Contents**—(*a*) The sailing instructions shall contain the following information:—

(i) That the race or races will be sailed under the rules of the

I.Y.R.U., the prescriptions of the National Authority, the sailing instructions and the rules of each class concerned.

(ii) The course or courses to be sailed or a list of **marks** or courses from which the course or courses will be selected, describing all **marks** and stating the order in which and the side on which each is to be rounded or passed.

(iii) The course signals.

(iv) The classes to race and class signals, if any.

(v) Time of start for each class.

(vi) Starting line and starting area if used.

(vii) Finishing line and any special instructions for shortening the course or for **finishing** a shortened course. (Where possible it is good practice for the sailing instructions for **finishing** a shortened course not to differ from those laid down for **finishing** the full course.)

(viii) Time limit, if any, for **finishing.**

(ix) Scoring system, if not previously announced in writing, including the method, if any, for breaking ties.

(*b*) The sailing instructions shall also cover such of the following matters as may be appropriate:—

(i) The date and place of the race or races.

(ii) When the race is to continue after sunset, the time or place, if any, at which the International Regulations for Preventing Collisions at Sea, or Government Right-of-Way Rules, shall replace the corresponding rules of Part IV, and the night signals the committee boat will display.

(iii) Any special instructions, subject to rule 3.1, which may vary or add to these rules, or class rules, and any special signals.

(iv) Eligibility: entry; measurement certificate; declaration.

(v) Any special instruction or signal, if any, regarding the carrying on board and wearing of personal buoyancy.

(vi) Names, national letters and distinguishing numbers and ratings, if any, of the yachts entered.

(vii) Any special instructions governing the methods of starting and recall.

(viii) Recall numbers or letters, if used, of the yachts entered.

(ix) Time allowances.

(x) Length of course or courses.

(xi) Method by which competitors will be notified of any change of course.

(xii) Information on tides and currents.

(xiii) Prizes.

(xiv) When rule 68.7, Alternative Penalties, if used, will apply.

(xv) Any special time limit within which, and address at which, a written protest shall be lodged, and the prescribed fee, if any, which shall accompany it.

(xvi) Time and place at which protests will be heard.

(xvii) That for the purpose of determining the result of a race which is one of a series of races in a competition, decisions of protests shall not be subject to appeal if it is essential to establish the results promptly.

(xviii) Whether races **postponed** or **abandoned** for the day will be sailed later and, if so, when and where.

(xix) Disposition to be made of a yacht appearing at the start alone in her class.

(xx) Time and place at which results of races will be posted.

3. **Distribution**—The sailing instructions shall be available to each yacht entitled to race.

4. **Changes**—The Race Committee may change the sailing instructions by notice, in writing if practicable, given to each yacht affected not later than the warning signal of her class.

5. **Oral Instructions**—Oral instructions shall not be given except in accordance with procedure specifically set out in the sailing instructions.

4—Signals

1. **International Code Flag Signals**—Unless otherwise prescribed in the sailing instructions, the following International Code flags shall be used as indicated and when displayed alone they shall apply to all classes, and when displayed over a class signal they shall apply to the designated class only:

"AP", Answering Pennant—Postponement Signal

(*a*) Means:—

"All races not started are **postponed.**

The warning signal will be made one minute after this signal is lowered."

(One sound signal shall be made with the lowering of the "AP".)

(*b*) Over one ball or shape, means:—

"The scheduled starting times of all races not started are **postponed** fifteen minutes."

(This postponement can be extended indefinitely by the addition of one ball or shape for every fifteen minutes.)

(*c*) Over one of the numeral pennants 1 to 9, means:—

"All races not started are **postponed** one hour, two hours, etc."

(*d*) Over the letter "A", means:—

"All races not started are **postponed** to a later date."

"B"—Protest signal.

When displayed by a yacht means:—

"I intend to lodge a protest."

"L"—Means:—

"Come within hail," or "Follow Me."

"M"—Mark Signal.

When displayed on a buoy, vessel, or other object, means:—

"Round or pass the object displaying this signal instead of the **mark** which it replaces."

"N"—Abandonment Signal.

Means:—

"All races are **abandoned.**"

"N over X"—Abandonment and Re-sail Signal.

Means:—

"All races are **abandoned** and will shortly be re-sailed.

Watch for fresh starting signals."

"N over First Repeater"—Cancellation Signal.

Means:—

"All races are **cancelled.**"

"P"—Preparatory Signal.

Means:—

"The class designated by the warning signal will **start** in 5 minutes exactly."

"R"—Reverse Course Signal.

Alone, means:—

"Sail the course prescribed in the sailing instructions in the reverse direction."

When displayed over a course signal, means:—

"Sail the designated course in the reverse direction."

"S"—Shorten Course Signal.

(*a*) at or near the starting line, means:—

"Sail the shortened course prescribed in the sailing instructions."

(*b*) at or near the finishing line, means:—

"**Finish** the race either:

(i) at the prescribed finishing line at the end of the round still to be completed by the leading yacht" or

(ii) "in any other manner prescribed in the sailing instructions under rule 3.2(*a*)(vii)."

(*c*) at or near a rounding **mark,** means:—

"**Finish** between the nearby **mark** and the committee boat."

"1st Repeater"—General Recall Signal.

Means:—

"The class is recalled for a fresh start as provided in sailing instructions."

2. **Signaling the Course**—The Race Committee shall either make the appropriate course signal or otherwise designate the course before or with the warning signal.

3. **Changing the Course**—The course for a class which has not **started** may be changed:—

(*a*) by displaying the appropriate **postponement** signal and indicating the new course before or with the warning signal to be displayed after the lowering of the **postponement** signal; or (*b*) by displaying a course signal or by removing and substituting a course signal before or with the warning signal.

(Method (*a*) is preferable when a change of course involves either shifting the committee boat or other starting **mark,** or requires a change of sails which cannot reasonably be completed within the five-minute period before the preparatory signal is made.)

4. **Signals for Starting a Race**

(*a*) Unless otherwise prescribed in the sailing instruction, the signals for starting a race shall be made at 5-minute intervals exactly, and shall be either:—

(i) *Warning Signal* —Class flag broken out or distinctive signal displayed.

Preparatory Signal —Code flag "P" broken out or distinctive signal displayed.

Starting Signal —Both warning and preparatory signals lowered.

In system (i) when classes are started:—

(*a*) at ten-minute intervals, the warning signal for each succeeding class shall be broken out or displayed at the starting signal of the preceding class, and

(*b*) at five-minute intervals, the preparatory signal for the first class to start shall be left flying or displayed until the last class has started. The warning signal for each succeeding class shall be broken out or displayed at the preparatory signal of the preceding class, or first class to start.

(ii) *Warning Signal* —White shape.
Preparatory Signal —Blue shape.
Starting Signal —Red shape.

In system (ii) each signal shall be lowered 30 seconds before the hoisting of the next, and in starting yachts by classes, the starting signal for each class shall be the preparatory signal for the next.

(*b*) Although rule 4.4(*a*) specifies 5-minute intervals between signals, this shall not interfere with the power of a Race Committee to start a series of races at any intervals which it considers desirable.

(*c*) A warning signal shall not be made before its scheduled time, except with the consent of all yachts entitled to race.

(*d*) When a significant error is made in the timing of the interval between any of the signals for starting a race, the recommended procedure is to have a general recall, **abandonment** or **postponement** of the race whose start is directly affected by the error and a corresponding **postponement** of succeeding races. Unless otherwise prescribed in the sailing instructions a new warning signal shall be made. When the race is not recalled, **abandoned** or **postponed** after an error in the timing of the interval, each succeeding

34

signal shall be made at the correct interval from the preceding signal.

5. **Finishing Signals**—Blue flag or shape. When displayed at the finish, means:—"The committee boat is on station at the finishing line."

6. **Other Signals**—The sailing instructions shall designate any other special signals and shall explain their meaning.

7. **Calling Attention to Signals**—Whenever the Race Committee makes a signal, except "R" or "S" before the warning signal, it shall call attention to its action as follows:—

Three guns or other sound signals when displaying "N", "N over X", or "N over 1st Repeater".

Two guns or other sound signals when displaying the "1st Repeater", "AP", or "S".

One gun or other sound signal when making any other signal, including the lowering of "AP" when the length of the postponement is not signaled.

8. **Visual Signal to Govern**—Times shall be taken from the visual starting signals, and a failure or mistiming of a gun or other sound signal shall be disregarded.

5—Cancelling, Postponing or Abandoning a Race and Changing or Shortening Course

1. The Race Committee:—

(*a*) before the starting signal may shorten the course or **cancel** or **postpone** a race for any reason, and

(*b*) after the starting signal may shorten the course by finishing a race at any rounding **mark** or **cancel** or **abandon** a race because of foul weather endangering the yachts, or because of insufficient wind, or because a **mark** is missing or has shifted or for other reasons directly affecting safety or the fairness of the competition.

(*c*) after the starting signal may change the course at any rounding **mark** subject to proper notice being given to each yacht as prescribed in the sailing instructions.

2. After a **postponement** the ordinary starting signals prescribed in rule 4.4(*a*) shall be used, and the postponement signal, if a general one, shall be hauled down before the first warning or course signal is made.

3. The Race Committee shall notify all yachts concerned by signal or otherwise when and where a race **postponed** or **abandoned** will be sailed.

6—Starting and Finishing Lines

The starting and finishing lines shall be either:—

(*a*) A line between a **mark** and a mast or staff on the committee boat or station clearly identified in the sailing instructions:

35

(*b*) a line between two **marks**; or

(*c*) the extension of a line through two stationary posts, with or without a **mark** at or near its outer limit, inside which the yachts shall pass.

For types (*a*) and (*c*) of starting or finishing lines the sailing instructions may also prescribe that a **mark** will be laid at or near the inner end of the line, in which case yachts shall pass between it and the outer **mark.**

7—Start of a Race

1. **Starting Area**—The sailing instructions may define a starting area which may be bounded by buoys; if so, they shall not rank as **marks.**

2. **Timing the Start**—The start of a yacht shall be timed from her starting signal.

8—Recalls

☆ 1. Yachts' sail numbers shall be used as recall numbers except that the Race Committee may instead allot a suitable recall number or letter to each yacht in accordance with rule 3.2(*b*)(viii).

2. When, at her starting signal, any part of a yacht's hull, crew or equipment is on the course side of the starting line or its extensions, or she is subject to rule 51.1(*c*), Sailing the Course, the Race Committee shall:

(*a*) when each yacht has been allotted a recall number or letter, display her recall number or letter as soon as possible and make a suitable sound signal. As soon as the recalled yacht has wholly returned to the pre-start side of the line or its extensions, the Race Committee shall so inform her by removing her recall number or letter. This is the preferred procedure.

(*b*) When no recall number or letter has been allotted, make a sound signal and leave the class warning signal at "the dip" or display such other signal as may be prescribed in the sailing instructions, until she has wholly returned to the pre-start side of the line or its extensions, or for such shorter period as the Race Committee considers reasonable.

The responsibility for returning shall rest with the yacht concerned.

(*c*) Follow such other procedure as may be prescribed in the sailing instructions.

3. (*a*) When there is either a number of unidentified premature starters, or an error in starting procedure, the Race Committee may make a general recall signal in accordance with rules 4.1, "First Repeater", and 4.7, Calling Attention to Signals. Unless otherwise prescribed in the sailing instructions, new warning and preparatory signals shall be made.

(*b*) Except as provided in rule 31.2, Disqualification, rule infringements before the preparatory signal for the new start shall be disregarded for the purpose of starting in the race to be re-started.

9—Marks

1. **Mark Missing**

(*a*) When any **mark** either is missing or has shifted, the Race Committee shall, if possible, replace it in its stated position, or substitute a new one with similar characteristics or a buoy or vessel displaying the letter "M" of the International Code—the **mark** signal.

(*b*) If it is impossible either to replace the **mark** or to substitute a new one in time for the yachts to round or pass it, the Race Committee may, at its discretion, act in accordance with rule 5.1, Cancelling, Postponing or Abandoning a Race and Changing or Shortening Course.

2. **Mark Unseen**—When races are sailed in fog or at night, dead reckoning alone should not necessarily be accepted as evidence that a **mark** has been rounded or passed.

10—Finishing Within a Time Limit

Unless otherwise prescribed in the sailing instructions, in races where there is a time limit, one yacht **finishing** within the prescribed limit shall make the race valid for all other yachts in that race.

11—Ties

When there is a tie at the finish of a race, either actual or on corrected times, the points for the place for which the yachts have tied and for the place immediately below shall be added together and divided equally. When two or more yachts tie for a trophy or prize in either a single race or a series, the yachts so tied shall, if practicable, sail a deciding race; if not, either the tie shall be broken by a method established under rule 3.2(*a*)(ix), or the yachts so tied shall either receive equal prizes or share the prize.

12—Yacht Materially Prejudiced

When, upon the request of a yacht made within the time limit provided by rule 68.3(*e*), Protests, or when the Race Committee, upon its own initiative, decides that, through no fault of her own, the finishing position of a yacht has been materially prejudiced: by rendering assistance in accordance with rule 58, Rendering Assistance; by being disabled by another yacht which was required to keep clear; or by an action or omission of the Race Committee; it may **cancel** or **abandon** the race or make such other arrangement as it deems equitable.

13—Races to be Re-sailed

When a race is to be re-sailed:—

1.   All yachts entered in the original race shall be eligible to **start** in the race to be re-sailed.

2.   Subject to the entry requirements of the original race, and at the discretion of the Race Committee, new entires may be accepted.

3.   Rule infringements in the original race shall be disregarded for the purpose of **starting** in the race to be re-sailed.

4.   The Race Committee shall notify the yachts concerned when and where the race will be re-sailed.

14—Award of Prizes, Places and Points

1.   Before awarding the prizes, the Race Committee shall be satisfied that all yachts whose finishing positions affect the awards have observed the racing rules, the prescriptions of the National Authority, the sailing instructions and the class rules.

2.   The sailing instructions may prescribe that in a particular instance the Race Committee may require the member in charge of a yacht to submit within a stated time limit a signed declaration to the effect that "all the racing rules, the prescriptions of the National Authority, the sailing instructions and the class rules were observed in the race (or races) on (date or dates of race or races)." A yacht which fails to observe the above requirement may, at the discretion of the Race Committee, be disqualified, or regarded as having retired.

(Numbers 15, 16, and 17 are spare numbers.)

PART III

GENERAL REQUIREMENTS
Owner's Responsibilities for Qualifying His Yacht

A yacht intending to **race** *shall, to avoid subsequent disqualification, comply with the rules of Part III before her preparatory signal and, when applicable, while* **racing.**

18—Entries

☆ Entries shall be made as required by the notice of the race or by the sailing instructions.

19—Measurement Certificates

1.   Every yacht entering a race shall hold such valid measurement or rating certificate as may be required by the National Authority or

other duly authorized body, by her class rules, by the notice of the race, or by the sailing instructions.

2. It shall be the owner's responsibility to maintain his yacht in the condition upon which her certifcate was based.

3. (a) If the owner of a yacht cannot produce such a certificate when required, he may be permitted to sign and lodge with the Race Committee, before she **starts,** a statement in the following form:

To the Secretary . . . . *Club*

UNDERTAKING TO PRODUCE CERTIFICATE

The yacht . . . . *competes in the* . . . . *race on condition that a valid certificate previously issued by the authorized administrative body, or a true copy of it, is submitted to the Race Committee before the end of the series, and that she competes in the race(s) on the measurement or rating of that certificate.*

Signed . . . .

(*Owner or his representative*)

Date . . . .

(b) In this event the sailing instructions may require that the owner shall lodge such a deposit as may be required by the National Authority, which may be forfeited if such certificate or true copy is not submitted to the Race Committee within the prescribed period.

20—Ownership of Yachts

1. Unless otherwise prescribed in the conditions of entry, a yacht shall be eligible to compete only when she is either owned by or on charter to and has been entered by a yacht or sailing club recognized by a National Authority or a member or members thereof.

2. Two or more yachts owned or chartered wholly or in part by the same body or person shall not compete in the same race without the previous consent of the Race Committee.

21—Member on Board

Every yacht shall have on board a member of a yacht or sailing club recognized by a National Authority to be in charge of the yacht as owner or owner's representative.

22—Shifting Ballast

1. **General Restrictions.** Floorboards shall be kept down; bulkheads and doors left standing; ladders, stairways and water tanks left in place; all cabin, galley and forecastle fixtures and fittings kept on board; all movable ballast shall be properly stowed under the floorboards or in lockers and no dead weight shall be shifted.

2. **Shipping, Unshipping or Shifting Ballast; Water.** No ballast,

whether movable or fixed, shall be shipped, unshipped or shifted, nor shall any water be taken in or discharged except for ordinary ship's use, from 2100 hours on the day before the race until the yacht is no longer **racing,** except that bilge water may be removed at any time.

3. **Clothing and Equipment.**

(*a*) A competitor shall not wear or carry any clothing or equipment for the purpose of increasing his weight.

(*b*) A class which desires to make exception to rule 22.3(*a*), Clothing and Equipment, may so prescribe in its class rules. In so doing, however, the total weight of clothing and equipment worn or carried by a competitor shall not exceed twenty kilograms when wet.

23—Anchor

Unless otherwise prescribed by her class rules, every yacht shall carry on board an anchor and chain or rope of suitable size.

24—Life-Saving Equipment

☆ Every yacht shall carry life-saving equipment conforming to government regulations for all persons on board, one item of which shall be ready for immediate use.

25—Class Emblems, National Letters and Distinguishing Numbers

1. Every yacht of an international class recognized by the I.Y.R.U. shall carry on her mainsail, or as provided in (*d*)(iii) and (iv) on her spinnaker:–

(*a*) An emblem, letter or number denoting the class to which she belongs.

(*b*) When **racing** in foreign waters a letter or letters showing her nationality, thus:–

A	Argentine	D	Denmark
AL	Algeria	DR	Dominican
AR	United Arab		Republic
	Republic	E	Spain
B	Belgium	EC	Ecuador
BA	Bahamas	F	France
BL	Brazil	G	Federal Re-
BU	Bulgaria		public of
CA	Cambodia		Germany
CB	Colombia	GO	German
CY	Republic of		Democratic
	Sri Lanka		Republic
CZ	Czechoslovakia	GR	Greece

40

GU	Guatemala	N	Norway
H	Holland	NK	Democratic
HA	Netherland		People's
	Antilles		Republic of
I	Italy		Korea
IL	Iceland	OE	Austria
IND	India	P	Portugal
IR	Republic of	PH	The
	Ireland		Philippines
IS	Israel	PK	Pakistan
J	Japan	PR	Puerto Rico
K	United	PU	Peru
	Kingdom	PZ	Poland
KA	Australia	RC	Cuba
KB	Bermuda	RI	Indonesia
KBA	Barbados	RM	Roumania
KC	Canada	S	Sweden
KG	Guyana	SA	Republic of
KGB	Gibraltar		South Africa
KH	Hong Kong	SE	Senegal
KJ	Jamaica	SL	El Salvador
KK	Kenya	SR	Union of
KR	Rhodesia		Soviet Socialist
KS	Singapore		Republics
KT	Trinidad	T	Tunisia
	and Tobago	TA	Republic of
KZ	New Zealand		China
KZA	Zambia		(Taiwan)
L	Finland	TH	Thailand
LE	Lebanon	TK	Turkey
LX	Luxembourg	U	Uruguay
M	Hungary	US	United States
MA	Morocco		of America
MG	Madagascar	V	Venezuela
MO	Monaco	VI	U.S. Virgin Islands
MT	Malta	X	Chile
MX	Mexico	Y	Yugoslavia
MY	Malaysia	Z	Switzerland

(c) Distinguishing number:–
A distinguishing number allotted to her by her National Authority. In the case of a self-administered international class, the number may be allotted by the class owners' association.
Assuming a Flying Dutchman yacht belonging to the Argentine Republic to be allotted number 3 by the Argentine National Authority, her sail shall be marked:

When there is insufficient space to place the letter or letters showing the yacht's nationality in front of her allotted number, it shall
be placed above the number.

(*d*) (i) The class emblems, letters or number, national letters and
distinguishing numbers shall be grouped so that the center of
the group is above half height; shall sharply contrast in color
with the sail; and shall be placed at different heights on the two
sides of the sail, those on the starboard side being uppermost, to
avoid confusion owing to translucency of the sail.

(ii) Where the class emblem, letter or number is of such a de-
sign that when placed back to back on the two sides of the sail
they coincide, they may be so placed.

(iii) When **racing** in foreign waters, the national letters and distinguishing numbers only shall be similarly placed on both
sides of the spinnaker, but at approximately half height.

(iv) When **racing** in home waters, the distinguishing numbers
only need be placed in accordance with rule 25.1(*d*)(iii).

(*e*) The following minimum sizes for national letters and distinguishing numbers are prescribed:–

Height: one-tenth of the measurement of the foot of the mainsail
rounded up to the nearest 50 mm.

Width: (excluding figure 1 and letter I) 70% of the height.

Thickness: 15% of the height.

Space between adjoining letters and numbers: 20% of the height.

Classes which have a variable sail plan shall specify in their class
rules the sizes of letters and numbers, which shall, if practicable,
conform to the above requirements.

☆ 2. (*a*) Unless otherwise authorized by the Race Committee or provided by class rules, a yacht not in one of the classes above shall carry
her class number, letter or emblem and her racing number on her
mainsail and spinnaker, as provided above, except that the only size
requirement may be as an alternative that the numbers, letters and
emblems shall be not less than 10 inches in height for yachts under 22
feet waterline length, not less than 15 inches in height for yachts 22
feet to 32 feet waterline and not less than 18 inches in height for
yachts over 32 feet waterline length.

☆ (*b*) Offshore racing yachts shall carry N.A.Y.R.U. numbers on main-
sails, spinnakers and all overlapping headsails whose LP measurement
exceeds 130%.

3. A yacht shall not be disqualified for infringing the provisions of
rule 25 without prior warning and adequate opportunity to make
correction.

26—Advertisements

1. The hull, crew or equipment of a yacht shall not display any form of advertisement except that:—

(*a*) One sailmaker's mark (which may include the name or mark of the manufacturer of the sail cloth) may be displayed on each side of any sail. The whole of such mark shall be placed not more than 15% of the length of the foot of the sail or 300 mm from its tack whichever is the greater. This latter limitation shall not apply to the position of marks on spinnakers.

(*b*) One builder's mark (which may include the name or mark of the designer) may be placed on the hull, and one maker's mark may be displayed on spars and equipment.

2. Marks (or plates) shall fit within a square not exceeding 150 mm x 150 mm (6 x 6 ins).

3. A yacht shall not be disqualified for infringing the provisions of this rule without prior warning and adequate opportunity to make correction.

27—Forestays and Jib Tacks

Unless otherwise prescribed in the class rules, forestays and jib tacks (excluding spinnaker staysails when not **close-hauled**) shall be fixed approximately in the center-line of the yacht.

28—Flags

☆ A yacht may display her private signal on the leech of her mainsail or from her mizzen mast head, and a wind indicator of a solid color or a feather. Other flags shall not be displayed except for signaling. A yacht shall not be disqualified for failing to comply with the provisions of this rule without warning and adequate opportunity to make correction.

(Numbers 29 and 30 are spare numbers)

PART IV

SAILING RULES WHEN YACHTS MEET
Helmsman's Rights and Obligations Concerning Right of Way

*The rules of Part IV apply only between yachts which either are intending to **race** or are **racing** in the same or different races, and, except when rule 3.2 (b)(ii) applies, replace the International Regulations for Preventing Collisions at Sea or Government Right-of-Way Rules applicable to the area concerned, from the time a yacht intending to **race** begins to sail about in the vi-*

43

cinity of the starting line until she has either **finished**
or retired and has left the vicinity of the course.

SECTION A—RULES WHICH ALWAYS APPLY

31—Disqualification

1. A yacht may be disqualified or otherwise penalized for infringing a rule of Part IV only when the infringement occurs while she is
racing, whether or not a collision results.

2. A yacht may be disqualified before or after she is **racing** for seriously hindering a yacht which is **racing,** or for infringing the sailing
instructions.

32—Avoiding Collisions

A right-of-way yacht which fails to make a reasonable attempt to
avoid a collision resulting in serious damage may be disqualified as
well as the other yacht.

33—Retiring from Race

A yacht which realizes she has infringed a racing rule or a sailing instruction is under an obligation to retire promptly; but, when she per-
sists in **racing,** other yachts shall continue to accord her such rights as
she may have under the rules of Part IV.

34—Right-of-Way Yacht Altering Course

When one yacht is required to keep clear of another, the right-of-
way yacht shall not so alter course as to prevent the other yacht from
keeping clear; so as to increase any alteration of course required of the
other yacht in order to keep clear; or so as to obstruct her while she is
keeping clear, except:

(*a*) to the extent permitted by rule 38.1, Right-of-Way Yacht Luffing after Starting, and

(*b*) when assuming a **proper course** to **start,** unless subject to the
second part of rule 44.1(*b*), Yachts Returning to Start.

35—Hailing

1. Except when **luffing** under rule 38.1, Luffing after Starting, a
right-of-way yacht which does not hail before or when making an alteration of course which may not be foreseen by the other yacht may
be disqualified as well as the yacht required to keep clear when a collision resulting in serious damage occurs.

2. A yacht which hails when claiming the establishment or termi-
nation of an **overlap** or insufficiency of room at a **mark** or **obstruction**
thereby helps to support her claim for the purposes of rule 42, Rounding or Passing Marks and Obstructions.

44

SECTION B—OPPOSITE TACK RULE

36—Fundamental Rule

A **port-tack** yacht shall keep clear of a **starboard-tack** yacht.

SECTION C—SAME TACK RULES

37—Fundamental Rules

1. A **windward yacht** shall keep clear of a **leeward yacht.**
2. A yacht **clear astern** shall keep clear of a yacht **clear ahead.**
3. A yacht which establishes an **overlap** to **leeward** from **clear a-stern** shall allow the **windward yacht** ample room and opportunity to keep clear, and during the existence of that **overlap** the **leeward yacht** shall not sail above her **proper course.**

38—Right-of-Way Yacht Luffing after Starting

1. **Luffing Rights and Limitations.** After she has **started** and cleared the starting line, a yacht **clear ahead** or a **leeward yacht** may **luff** as she pleases, except that:—

A **leeward yacht** shall not sail above her **proper course** while an **overlap** exists if, at any time during its existence, the helmsman of the **windward yacht** (when sighting abeam from his normal **station** and sailing no higher than the **leeward yacht**) has been abreast or forward of the mainmast of the **leeward yacht.**

2. **Overlap Limitations.** For the purpose of this rule: An **overlap** does not exist unless the yachts are clearly within two overall lengths of the longer yacht; and an **overlap** which exists between two yachts when the leading yacht **starts,** or when one or both of them completes a **tack** or **jibe,** shall be regarded as a new **overlap** beginning at that time.

3. **Hailing to Stop or Prevent a Luff.** When there is doubt, the **lee-ward yacht** may assume that she has the right to **luff** unless the helms-man of the **windward yacht** has hailed "Mast Abeam", or words to that effect. The **leeward yacht** shall be governed by such hail, and, if she deems it improper, her only remedy is to protest.

4. **Curtailing a Luff.** The **windward yacht** shall not cause a **luff** to be curtailed because of her proximity to the **leeward yacht** unless an **obstruction,** a third yacht or other object restricts her ability to re-spond.

5. **Luffing Two or More Yachts.** A yacht shall not **luff** unless she has the right to **luff** all yachts which would be affected by her **luff,** in which case they shall all respond even if an intervening yacht or yachts would not otherwise have the right to **luff.**

39—Sailing Below a Proper Course

A yacht which is on a free leg of the course shall not sail below her **proper course** when she is clearly within three of her overall lengths of either a **leeward yacht** or a yacht **clear astern** which is steering a course to pass to **leeward.**

40—Right-of-Way Yacht Luffing before Starting

Before a yacht has **started** and cleared the starting line, any **luff** on her part which causes another yacht to have to alter course to avoid a collision shall be carried out slowly and in such a way so as to give the **windward yacht** room and opportunity to keep clear, but the **leeward yacht** shall not so **luff** above a **close-hauled** course, unless the helmsman of the **windward yacht** (sighting abeam from his normal station) is abaft the mainmast of the **leeward yacht.** Rules 38.3, Hailing to Stop or Prevent a Luff; 38.4, Curtailing a Luff; and 38.5, Luffing Two or More Yachts, also apply.

SECTION D—CHANGING TACK RULES

41—Tacking or Jibing

1.   A yacht which is either **tacking** or **jibing** shall keep clear of a yacht **on a tack.**

2.   A yacht shall neither **tack** nor **jibe** into a position which will give her right of way unless she does so far enough from a yacht **on a tack** to enable this yacht to keep clear without having to begin to alter her course until after the **tack** or **jibe** has been completed.

3.   A yacht which **tacks** or **jibes** has the onus of satisfying the Race Committee that she completed her **tack** or **jibe** in accordance with rule 41.2.

4.   When two yachts are both **tacking** or both **jibing** at the same time, the one on the other's **port** side shall keep clear.

SECTION E—RULES OF EXCEPTION
AND SPECIAL APPLICATION

When a rule of this section applies, to the extent to which it explicitly provides rights and obligations, it over-rides any conflicting rule of Part IV which precedes it except the rules of Section A—Rules Which Always Apply.

42—Rounding or Passing Marks and Obstructions

1.   **Fundamental Rules Regarding Room.** When yachts either on the same **tack** or, after **starting** and clearing the starting line, on opposite **tacks,** are about to round or pass a **mark** on the same required

46

side, with the exception of a starting **mark** surrounded by navigable water, or an **obstruction** on the same side:—

(*a*) When **Overlapped:**

   (i) An outside yacht shall give each yacht **overlapping** her on the inside, room to round or pass the **mark** or **obstruction,** except as provided in rules 42.1(*a*)(iii), and (iv) and 42.3. Room includes room for an **overlapping** yacht to **tack** or **jibe** when either is an integral part of the rounding or passing maneuver.

   (ii) When an inside yacht of two or more **overlapped** yachts either on opposite **tacks,** or on the same **tack** without **luffing** rights, will have to **jibe** in order most directly to assume a **proper course** to the next **mark,** she shall **jibe** at the first reasonable opportunity.

   (iii) When two yachts on opposite **tacks** are on a **beat** or when one of them will have to **tack** either to round the **mark** or to avoid the **obstruction,** as between each other, rule 42.1(*a*)(i) shall not apply and they are subject to rules 36, Opposite Tack Fundamental Rule, and 41, Tacking or Jibing.

   (v) An outside **leeward yacht** with luffing rights may take an inside yacht to windward of a **mark** provided that she hails to that effect and begins to **luff** before she is within two of her overall lengths of the **mark** and provided that she also passes to windward of it.

(*b*) When **Clear Astern** and **Clear Ahead:**

   (i) A yacht **clear astern** shall keep clear in anticipation of and during the rounding or passing maneuver when the yacht **clear ahead** remains on the same **tack** or **jibes.**

   (ii) A yacht **clear ahead** which **tacks** to round a **mark** is subject to rule 41, Tacking or Jibing, but a yacht **clear astern** shall not **luff** above **close-hauled** so as to prevent the yacht **clear ahead** from **tacking.**

2. **Restrictions on Establishing and Maintaining an Overlap**

(*a*) A yacht **clear astern** shall not establish an inside **overlap** and be entitled to room under rule 42.1(*a*)(i) when the yacht **clear ahead:**—

   (i) is within two of her overall lengths of the **mark** or **obstruction,** except as provided in rules 42.2(*b*) and 42.2(*c*), or

   (ii) is unable to give the required room.

(*b*) The two-lengths determinative above shall not apply to yachts, of which one has completed a **tack** within two overall lengths of a **mark** or an **obstruction.**

(*c*) A yacht **clear astern** may establish an **overlap** between the yacht **clear ahead** and a continuing **obstruction** such as a shoal or the shore only when there is room for her to do so in safety.

(*d*) (i) A yacht **clear ahead** shall be under no obligation to give room to a yacht **clear astern** before an **overlap** is established.

(ii) A yacht which claims an inside **overlap** has the onus of satisfying the Race Committee that the **overlap** was established in proper time.

(*e*) (i) When an outside yacht is **overlapped** at the time she comes within two of her overall lengths of a **mark**, or an **obstruction**, she shall continue to be bound by rule 42.1(*a*)(i) to give room as required even though the **overlap** may thereafter be broken.

(ii) An outside yacht which claims to have broken an **overlap** has the onus of satisfying the Race Committee that she became **clear ahead** when she was more than two of her overall lengths from the **mark** or an **obstruction**.

3. **At a Starting Mark Surrounded by Navigable Water**

When approaching the starting line to **start**, a **leeward yacht** shall be under no obligation to give any **windward yacht** room to pass to leeward of a starting **mark** surrounded by navigable water; but, after the starting signal, a **leeward yacht** shall not deprive a **windward yacht** of room at such a **mark** by sailing either above the course to the first **mark** or above **close-hauled**.

43—Close-Hauled, Hailing for Room to Tack at Obstructions

1. **Hailing.** When two **close-hauled** yachts are on the same **tack** and safe pilotage requires the yacht **clear ahead** or the **leeward yacht** to make a substantial alteration of course to clear an **obstruction**, and if she intends to **tack**, but cannot **tack** without colliding with the other yacht, she shall hail the other yacht for room to **tack** and clear the other yacht, but she shall not hail and **tack** simultaneously.

2. **Responding.** The hailed yacht at the earliest possible moment after the hail shall either:—

(*a*) **tack**, in which case, the hailing yacht shall begin to **tack** either:—

(i) before the hailed yacht has completed her **tack**,

(ii) if she cannot then **tack** without colliding with the hailed yacht, immediately she is able to **tack** and clear her, or

(*b*) reply "You **tack**", or words to that effect, if in her opinion she can keep clear without **tacking** or after postponing her **tack**. In this case:—

(i) the hailing yacht shall immediately **tack** and

(ii) the hailed yacht shall keep clear.

(iii) The onus shall lie on the hailed yacht which replied "You **tack**" to satisfy the Race Committee that she kept clear.

3. **Limitation on Right to Room when the Obstruction is a Mark.**

(*a*) When the hailed yacht can fetch an **obstruction** which is also a **mark** the hailing yacht shall not be entitled to room to **tack** and clear the other yacht and the hailed yacht shall immediately so inform the hailing yacht.

(*b*) If, thereafter, the hailing yacht again hails for room to **tack** and clear the other yacht she shall, after receiving it, retire immediately.

(*c*) If, after having refused to respond to a hail under rule 43.3(*a*), the hailed yacht fails to fetch, she shall retire immediately.

44—Yachts Returning to Start

1. (*a*) A premature starter when returning to **start,** or a yacht working into position from the course side of the starting line or its extensions, when the starting signal is made, shall keep clear of all yachts which are **starting,** or have **started,** correctly, until she is wholly on the pre-start side of the starting line or its extensions.

(*b*) Thereafter, she shall be accorded the rights under the rules of Part IV of a yacht which is **starting** correctly; but if she thereby acquires right of way over another yacht which is **starting** correctly, she shall allow that yacht ample room and opportunity to keep clear.

2. A premature starter while continuing to sail the course and until it is obvious that she is returning to **start,** shall be accorded the rights under the rules of Part IV of a yacht which has **started.**

45—Yachts Re-rounding after Touching a Mark

1. A yacht which has touched a **mark** and is about to exonerate herself in accordance with rule 52.2, Touching a Mark, shall keep clear of all other yachts which are about to round or pass it or have rounded or passed it correctly, until she has rounded it completely and has cleared it and is on a **proper course** to the next **mark.**

2. A yacht which has touched a **mark,** while continuing to sail the course and until it is obvious that she is returning to round it completely in accordance with rule 52.2, Touching a Mark, shall be accorded rights under the rules of Part IV.

SECTION F—WHEN NOT UNDER WAY

46—Anchored, Aground or Capsized

1. A yacht under way shall keep clear of another yacht **racing** which is anchored, aground or capsized. Of two anchored yachts, the one which anchored later shall keep clear, except that a yacht which is dragging shall keep clear of one which is not.

2. A yacht anchored or aground shall indicate the fact to any yacht which may be in danger of fouling her. Unless the size of the yachts or the weather conditions make some other signal necessary a hail is sufficient indication.

3. A yacht shall not be penalized for fouling a yacht in distress

which she is attempting to assist or a yacht which goes aground or capsizes immediately ahead of her

(Numbers 47 and 48 are spare numbers.)

OTHER SAILING RULES
Obligations of Helmsman and Crew in Handling a Yacht

*Except for rule 49, a yacht is subject to the rules of Part V only while she is **racing**.*

49—Fair Sailing

A yacht shall attempt to win a race only by fair sailing, superior speed and skill, and, except in team races, by individual effort. However, a yacht may be disqualified under this rule only in the case of a clear-cut violation of the above principles and only if no other rule applies.

50—Ranking as a Starter

A yacht whose entry has been accepted by the Race Committee and which sails about in the vicinity of the starting line between her preparatory and starting signals shall rank as a starter, even if she does not **start**.

51—Sailing the Course

1.   (*a*) A yacht shall **start** and **finish** only as prescribed in the starting and finishing definition.
(*b*) Unless otherwise prescribed in the sailing instructions, a yacht which either crosses prematurely, or is on the course side of the starting line, or its extensions, at the starting signal, shall return and **start** in accordance with the definition.
(*c*) Unless otherwise prescribed in the sailing instructions, when after a general recall, any part of a yacht's hull, crew or equipment is on the course side of the starting line or its extensions during the minute before her starting signal, she shall thereafter return to the pre-start side of the line across one of its extensions and **start.**
(*d*) Failure of a yacht to see or hear her recall notification shall not relieve her of her obligation to **start** correctly.
2.   A yacht shall sail the course so as to round or pass each **mark** on the required side in correct sequence, and so that a string representing

her wake from the time she **starts** until she **finishes** would, when drawn taut, lie on the required side of each **mark.**

3. A **mark** has a required side for a yacht as long as she is on a leg which it begins, bounds or ends. A starting line **mark** begins to have a required side for a yacht when she **starts.** A starting limit **mark** has a required side for a yacht from the time she is approaching the starting line to **start** until she has left it astern on the first leg. A finishing line **mark** and a finishing limit **mark** cease to have a required side for a yacht as soon as she **finishes.**

4. A yacht which rounds or passes a **mark** on the wrong side may exonerate herself by making her course conform to the requirements of rule 51.2.

5. It is not necessary for a yacht to cross the finishing line completely; after **finishing** she may clear it in either direction.

☆ 6. In the absence of the Race Committee, a yacht shall take her own time when she finishes, and report the time taken to the Race Committee as soon as possible. If there is no longer an established finishing line, the finishing line shall be a line extending from the required side of the finishing **mark** at right angles to the last leg of the course, and 100 yards long or as much longer as may be necessary to insure adequate depth of water in crossing it.

52—Touching a Mark

1. A yacht which either:—

   (*a*) touches:—

      (i) a starting **mark** before **starting:**

      (ii) a **mark** which begins, bounds or ends the leg of the course on which she is sailing: or

      (iii) a finishing **mark** after **finishing,** or

   (*b*) causes a **mark** or **mark** vessel to shift to avoid being touched, shall immediately retire, unless either:

      (i) she alleges that she was wrongfully compelled by another yacht to touch it or cause it to shift, in which case she shall protest; or

      (ii) she exonerates herself in accordance with rule 52.2.

2. (*a*) Unless otherwise prescribed in the sailing instructions, a yacht which touches a **mark** surrounded by navigable water may exonerate herself by completing one entire rounding of the **mark,** leaving it on the required side, and thereafter she shall re-round or re-pass it, without touching it, as required to sail the course in accordance with rule 51, Sailing the Course, and the sailing instructions.

   (*b*) When a yacht touches:

      (i) starting **mark,** she shall carry out the rounding after she has **started;** or

(ii) a finishing **mark,** she shall carry out the rounding, and she shall not rank as having **finished** until she has completed the rounding and again crosses the finishing line in accordance with the definition of **finishing.**

53—Fog Signals and Lights

1.   Every yacht shall observe the International Regulations for Preventing Collisions at Sea or Government Rules and fog signals and, as a minimum, the carrying of lights at night.

2.   The use of additional special purpose lights such as masthead, spreader or jib luff lights shall not constitute grounds for protest.

54—Setting and Sheeting Sails

1.   **Changing Sails.** While changing headsails and spinnakers a replacing sail may be fully set and trimmed before the sail it replaces is taken in, but only one mainsail and, except when changing, only one spinnaker shall be carried set.

2.   **Sheeting Sails to Spars.** Unless otherwise prescribed by the class rules, any sail may be sheeted to or led above a boom regularly used for a working sail and permanently attached to the mast to which the head of the working sail is set, but no sails shall be sheeted over or through outriggers. An outrigger is any fitting so placed, except as permitted in the first sentence of rule 54.2, that it could exert outward pressure on a sheet at a point from which, with the yacht upright, a vertical line would fall outside the hull or deck planking at that point, or outside such other position as class rules prescribe. For the purpose of this rule: bulwarks, rails and rubbing strakes are not part of the hull or deck planking. A boom of a boomed headsail which requires no adjustment when **tacking** is not an outrigger.

3.   **Spinnaker, Spinnaker Pole.** A spinnaker shall not be set without a pole. The tack of a spinnaker when set and drawing shall be in close proximity to the outboard end of a spinnaker pole. Any headsail may be attached to a spinnaker pole provided a spinnaker is not set. A sail tacked down abaft the foremost mast is not a headsail. Only one spinnaker pole shall be used at a time and when in use shall be carried only on the side of the foremost mast opposite to the main boom and shall be fixed to the mast. Rule 54.3 shall not apply when shifting a spinnaker pole or sail attached thereto.

55—Owner Steering Another Yacht

An owner shall not steer any yacht other than his own in a race wherein his own yacht competes, without the previous consent of the Race Committee.

56—Boarding

Unless otherwise prescribed in the sailing instructions, no person shall board a yacht except for the purpose of rule 58, Rendering Assistance, or to attend an injured or ill member of the crew or temporarily as one of the crew of a vessel fouled.

57—Leaving, Man Overboard

Unless otherwise prescribed in the sailing instructions, no person on board a yacht when her preparatory signal was made shall leave, unless injured or ill, or for the purposes of rule 58, Rendering Assistance, except that any member of the crew may fall overboard or leave her to swim, stand on the bottom as a means of anchoring, haul her out ashore to effect repairs, reef sails or bail out, or help her to get clear after grounding or fouling another vessel or object, provided that this person is back on board before the yacht continues in the race.

58—Rendering Assistance

Every yacht shall render all possible assistance to any vessel or person in peril, when in a position to do so.

59—Outside Assistance

Except as permitted by rules 56, Boarding, 58, Rendering Assistance, and 64, Aground or Foul of an Obstruction, a yacht shall neither receive outside assistance nor use any gear other than that on board when her preparatory signal was made.

60—Means of Propulsion

A yacht shall be propelled only by the natural action of the wind on the sails, spars and hull, and water on the hull, and shall not pump, "ooch" or rock, as described in Appendix 2, nor check way by abnormal means, except for the purpose of rule 58, Rendering Assistance, or of recovering a man who has accidentally fallen overboard. An oar, paddle or other object may be used in emergency for steering. An anchor may be sent out in a boat only as permitted by rule 64, Aground or Foul of an Obstruction.

61—Sounding

Any means of sounding may be used provided rule 60, Means of Propulsion, is not infringed.

62—Manual Power

A yacht shall use manual power only, except that a power winch or windlass may be used in weighing anchor or in getting clear after running aground or fouling any object, and a power bilge pump may be used in an auxiliary yacht.

63—Anchoring and Making Fast

1.   A yacht may anchor. Means of anchoring may include the crew standing on the bottom and any weight lowered to the bottom. A yacht shall recover any anchor or weight used, and any chain or rope attached to it, before continuing in the race, unless after making every effort she finds recovery impossible. In this case she shall report the circumstances to the Race Committee, which may disqualify her if it considers the loss due either to inadequate gear or to insufficient effort to recover it.

2.   A yacht shall be afloat and off moorings, before her preparatory signal, but may be anchored, and shall not thereafter make fast or be made fast by means other than anchoring, nor be hauled out, except for the purpose of rule 64, Aground or Foul of an Obstruction, or to effect repairs, reef sails or bail out.

64—Aground or Foul of an Obstruction

A yacht, after grounding or fouling another vessel or other object, is subject to rule 62, Manual Power, and may, in getting clear, use her own anchors, boats, ropes, spars and other gear; may send out an anchor in a boat; may be refloated by her crew going overboard either to stand on the bottom or to go ashore to push off; but may receive outside assistance only from the crew of the vessel fouled. A yacht shall recover all her own gear used in getting clear before continuing in the race.

65—Skin Friction

A yacht shall not eject or release from a container any substance (such as polymer) the purpose of which is, or could be, to reduce the frictional resistance of the hull by altering the character of the flow of water inside the boundary layer.

66—Increasing Stability

Unless otherwise prescribed by her class rules or in the sailing instructions, a yacht shall not use any device, such as a trapeze or plank, to project outboard the weight of any of the crew, nor, when a yacht is equipped with lifelines, shall any member of the crew station any part of his torso outside them, other than temporarily.

PART VI

PROTESTS, DISQUALIFICATIONS AND APPEALS

67—Contact between Yachts Racing

1.   When there is contact between the hull, spars, standing rigging or crew of two yachts while racing, both shall be disqualified, unless one of them retires in acknowledgement of an infringement of the rules, or one or both of them acts in accordance with rule 68.3, Protests.

2.   A third yacht which witnesses an apparent collision between two yachts and, after finishing or retiring, discovers that neither of them has observed rule 67.1, is relieved by rule 68.3(*b*) from the requirement of showing a protest flag and may lodge a protest against them.

3.   The race committee may waive this rule when it is satisfied that minor contact was unavoidable.

68—Protests

1.   A yacht can protest against any other yacht, except that a protest for an alleged infringement of the rules of Part IV can be made only by a yacht directly involved in, or witnessing an incident.

2.   A protest occurring between yachts competing in separate races sponsored by different clubs shall be heard by a combined committee of both clubs.

3.   (*a*) A protest for an infringement of the rules or sailing instructions occurring during a race shall be signified by showing a flag (International Code flag "B" is always acceptable, irrespective of any other provisions in the sailing instructions) conspicuously in the rigging of the protesting yacht at the first reasonable opportunity and keeping it flying until she has **finished** or retired, or if the first reasonable opportunity occurs after **finishing,** until acknowledged by the Race Committee. In the case of a yacht sailed singlehanded, it will be sufficient if the flag (whether displayed in the rigging or not) is brought to the notice of the yacht protested against as soon as possible after the incident and to the Race Committee when the protesting yacht **finishes.**

(*b*) A yacht which has no knowledge of the facts justifying a protest until after she has **finished** or retired may nevertheless protest without having shown a protest flag.

(*c*) A protesting yacht shall try to inform the yacht protested against that a protest will be lodged.

(*d*) Such a protest shall be in writing and be signed by the owner or his representative, and include the following particulars:

   (i) The date, time and whereabouts of the incident.

   (ii) The particular rule or rules or sailing instructions alleged to have been infringed.

(iii) A statement of the facts.

(iv) Unless irrelevant, a diagram of the incident.

(*e*) Unless otherwise prescribed in the sailing instructions a protesting yacht shall deliver, or if that is not possible, mail her protest to the Race Committee:

(i) within two hours of the time she **finishes** the race, or within such time as may have been prescribed in the sailing instructions under rule 3.2(*b*)(xv), unless the Race Committee has reason to extend these time limits, or

(ii) when she does not **finish** the race, within such a time as the Race Committee may consider reasonable in the circumstances of the case. A protest shall be accompanied by such fee, if any, as may have been prescribed in the sailing instructions under rule 3.2(*b*)(xv).

(*f*) The Race Committee shall allow the protestor to remedy at a later time:

(i) any defects in the details required by rule 68.3(*d*) provided that the protest includes a summary of the facts, and

(ii) a failure to deposit such fee as may be required under rule 68.3(*c*) and prescribed in the sailing instructions.

4. (*a*) A protest that a measurement, scantling or flotation rule has been infringed while **racing,** or that a classification or rating certificate is for any reason invalid, shall be lodged with the Race Committee not later than 1800 hours on the day following the race. The Race Committee shall send a copy of the protest to the yacht protested against and, when there appears to be reasonable grounds for the protest, it shall refer the question to an authority qualified to decide such questions. (See Appendix 6)

(*b*) Deviations in excess of tolerances stated in the class rules caused by normal wear or damage and which do not affect the performance of the yacht shall not invalidate the measurement or rating certificate of the yacht for a particular race, but shall be rectified before she races again, unless in the opinion of the Race Committee there has been no practical opportunity to rectify the wear or damage.

(*c*) The Race Committee, in making its decision, shall be governed by the determination of such authority. Copies of such decision shall be sent to all yachts involved.

5. (*a*) A yacht which alleges that her chances of winning a prize have been prejudiced by an action or omission of the Race Committee, may seek redress from the Race Committee in accordance with the requirements for a protest provided in rules 68.3(*d*), (*e*) and (*f*). In these circumstances a protest flag need not be shown.

(*b*) When the Race Committee decides that such action or omission was prejudicial, and that the result of the race was altered thereby, it shall cancel or **abandon** the race, or make such other arrangement as it deems equitable.

6. A protest made in writing shall not be withdrawn, but shall be decided by the Race Committee, unless prior to the hearing full responsibility is acknowledged by one or more yachts.

7. Alternative Penalties. When so prescribed in the sailing instructions, the procedure and penalty for infringing a rule of Part IV shall be as provided in Appendix 3, Alternative Penalties for Infringement of a Rule of Part IV.

69—Refusal of a Protest

1. When the Race Committee decides that a protest does not conform to the requirements of rule 68, Protests, it shall inform the protesting yacht that her protest will not be heard and of the reasons for such decision.

2. Such a decision shall not be reached without giving the protesting yacht all opportunity of bringing evidence that the requirements of rule 68, Protests, were complied with.

70—Hearings

1. When the Race Committee decides that a protest conforms to all the requirements of rule 68, Protests, it shall call a hearing as soon as possible. The protest, or a copy of it, shall be made available to all yachts involved, and each shall be notified, in writing if practicable, of the time and place set for the hearing. A reasonable time shall be allowed for the preparation of defense. At the hearing, the Race Committee shall take the evidence presented by the parties to the protest and such other evidence as it may consider necessary. The parties to the protest, or a representative of each, shall have the right to be present, but all others, except one witness at a time while testifying, may be excluded. A yacht other than one named in the protest, which is involved in that protest, shall have all the rights of yachts originally named in it.

2. A yacht shall not be penalized without a hearing, except as provided in rule 73.1(*a*), Disqualification without Protest.

3. Failure on the part of any of the interested parties or a representative to make an effort to attend the hearing of the protest may justify the Race Committee in deciding the protest as it thinks fit without a full hearing.

71—Decisions

The Race Committee shall make its decision promptly after the hearing. Each decision shall be communicated to the parties involved, and shall state fully the facts and grounds on which it is based and shall specify the rules, if any, infringed. If requested by any of the parties, such decision shall be given in writing and shall include the Race Committee's diagram. The findings of the Race Committee as to the facts involved shall be final.

72—Disqualification after Protest

1. When the Race Committee, after hearing a protest or acting under rule 73, Disqualification without Protest, or any appeal authority, is satisfied:—

(*a*) that a yacht has infringed any of these rules or the sailing instructions, or

(*b*) that in consequence of her neglect of any of these rules or the sailing instructions she has compelled other yachts to infringe any of these rules or the sailing instructions,

she shall be disqualified unless the sailing instructions applicable to that race provide some other penalty. Such disqualification or other penalty shall be imposed, irrespective of whether the rule or sailing instruction which led to the disqualification or penalty was mentioned in the protest, or the yacht which was at fault was mentioned or protested against, e.g., the protesting yacht or a third yacht might be disqualified and the protested yacht absolved.

2. For the purpose of awarding points in a series, a retirement after an infringement of any of these rules or the sailing instructions shall not rank as a disqualification. This penalty can be imposed only in accordance with rules 72, Disqualification after Protest, and 73, Disqualification without Protest.

3. When a yacht either is disqualified or has retired, the next in order shall be awarded her place.

73—Disqualification without Protest

1. (*a*) A yacht which fails either to **start** or to **finish** may be disqualified without protest or hearing, after the conclusion of the race, except that she shall be entitled to a hearing, provided she satisfies the Race Committee that an error may have been made.

(*b*) A yacht so penalized shall be informed of the action taken, either by letter or by notification in the racing results.

2. When the Race Committee:—

(*a*) sees an apparent infringement by a yacht of any of these rules or the sailing instructions (except as provided in rule 73.1), or

(*b*) has reasonable grounds for believing that an infringement resulted in serious damage, or

(*c*) receives a report not later than the same day from a witness who was neither competing in the race, nor otherwise an interested party, alleging an infringement, or

(*d*) has reasonable grounds for supposing from the evidence at the hearing of a valid protest, that any yacht involved in the incident may have committed such an infringement, it may notify such yacht thereof orally, or if that is not possible, in writing, delivered or mailed not later than 1800 hours on the day after:—

(i) the finish of the race, or

(ii) the receipt of the report, or

(iii) the hearing of the protest.

Such notice shall contain a statement of the pertinent facts and of the particular rule or rules or sailing instructions believed to have been infringed, and the Race Committee shall act thereon in the same manner as if it had been a protest made by a competitor.

74—Penalties for Gross Infringement of Rules

1. When a gross infringement of any of these rules, the sailing instructions or class rules is proved against the owner, the owner's representative, the helmsman or sailing master of a yacht, such persons may be disqualified by the National Authority, for any period it may think fit, from either steering or sailing in a yacht in any race held under its jurisdiction.

2. Notice of any penalty adjudged under this rule shall be communicated to the I.Y.R.U. which shall inform all National Authorities.

3. After a gross breach of good manners or sportsmanship the Race Committee may exclude a competitor from further participation in a series or take other disciplinary action.

75—Persons Interested Not to Take Part in Decision

1. No member of either a Race Committee or of any appeals authority shall take part in the discussion or decision upon any disputed question in which he is an interested party, but this does not preclude him from giving evidence in such a case.

2. The term "interested party" includes anyone who stands to gain or lose as a result of the decision.

76—Expenses Incurred by Protest

Unless otherwise prescribed by the Race Committee, the fees and expenses entailed by a protest on measurement or classification shall be paid by the unsuccessful party.

77—Appeals

☆ 1. **Limitations on Right to Appeal**—Appeals involving solely the interpretation of the racing rules may be taken to the Appeals Committee of the Union for final determination:

(*a*) If the Club is a member of the Union but is not a member of a local association or district belonging to the Union, by an owner or his representative from a decision of the Race Committee.

(*b*) If the Club is a member of a local association or district belonging to the Union by an owner or his representative or by the

Race Committee from a decision of the local association or district.

2. **Appeal Procedure**—(*a*) A notice of appeal shall be mailed, not later than ten days from receipt of the written decision, to the body rendering the decision, preferably with a copy to the Appeals Committee, and shall contain the grounds for the appeal, that is to say, how the appellant believes the rules should be interpreted and his reasons therefor.

(*b*) The body rendering the decision shall promptly notify the other parties involved, sending them a copy of the notice of appeal.

(*c*) In an appeal to the Union the body rendering the decision shall promptly file, in writing, with the Secretary of the Union all particulars called for by rule 78, Particulars to be Supplied in Appeals.

3. **Decision of Appeals Committee**—Decisions of the Appeals Committee shall be in writing and the grounds of each decision shall be specified therein. Each decision shall be filed with the Secretary of the Union, who shall send copies thereof to all parties to the infringement and appeal.

78—Particulars to be Supplied in Appeals

☆ An appeal to the Union shall include the following particulars so far as they are applicable:

1. A copy of the protest or protests, request for relief or statement by the Race Committee acting under rule 73.2, as the case may be, together with all other written statements which may have been put in by the parties.

2. The names or numbers of the yachts represented at the hearing, and of any yacht duly notified of the hearing, but not represented, and the name and address of the representative of each of said yachts.

3. A copy of the sailing instructions.

4. A copy of the decision of the Race Committee containing a full statement of the facts found by it, its decision and the grounds therefor.

5. An official diagram prepared by the Race Committee in accordance with the facts found by it and signed by it and showing (i) the course to the next **mark** or, if close by, the **mark** itself and its required side, (ii) the direction and velocity of the wind, (iii) the set of the current, if any, and (iv) the position or positions and tracks of the yachts involved.

6. A copy of the decision, if any, of the local association or district.

7. A copy of the notice of appeal, including the grounds thereof.

8. Observations, if any, upon the appeal by any of the parties.

79—Questions of Interpretation

☆ The Appeals Committee will accept and act upon questions involving solely the interpretation of the racing rules but only when submitted by a club or local association or district, from whose decision an appeal may be taken as provided in rule 77.1, Limitations on Right to Appeal. Decisions of such questions may, at the discretion of the Chairman of the Appeals Committee, be acted upon by less than the full committee. Questions should include all the assumed facts, an assumed sailing instruction if pertinent, and a diagram if one will help to clarify the facts. Questions are not acceptable on protest decisions which may be appealed.

TEAM RACING RULES

Team racing shall be sailed under the yacht racing rules of the International Yacht Racing Union as adopted by the North American Yacht Racing Union supplemented as follows:

SAILING RULES

1. A yacht may maneuver against a yacht sailing on another leg of the course only if she can do so while sailing a **proper course** relative to the leg on which she herself is sailing. For the purpose of this rule, each time a leg is sailed it shall be regarded as "another leg of the course".

2. Except to protect her own or a team mate's finishing position, a yacht in one team which is completing the last leg of the course shall not maneuver against a yacht in another team which has no opponent astern of her.

3. Right of way may be waived by team mates, provided that in so doing, I.Y.R.U. rule 34, Right-of-Way Yacht Altering Course, is not infringed in respect to an opponent; but if contact occurs between them and neither retires immediately, the poorer finishing team mate shall automatically be disqualified.

The benefits of rule 12, Yacht Materially Prejudiced, shall not be available to a yacht damaged by contact between team mates.

4. When two **overlapping** yachts on the same **tack** are in the act of rounding or passing on the required side of a **mark** at which their **proper course** changes:

   (a) If the **leeward yacht** is inside, she may, if she has **luffing** rights, hold her course or **luff**. If she does not have **luffing** rights, she shall promptly assume her **proper course** to the next **mark** whether or not she has to **jibe**.

   (b) If the **windward yacht** is inside, she shall promptly **luff** up to her **proper course** to the next **mark**, or if she cannot assume such

61

proper course without **tacking** and does not choose to **tack,** she shall promptly **luff** up to **close-hauled.** This clause does not restrict a **leeward yacht's** right to **luff** under rule 38, Luffing after Starting.

SCORING

5. **Each Race**

(a) Yachts shall score three-quarters of a point for first place, two points for second place, three points for third place, and so on.

(b) A yacht which does not **start** shall score points equal to the number of yachts entitled to **start** in the race.

(c) A yacht which infringes any rule and retires with reasonable promptness shall score one point more than the number of yachts entitled to **start** in the race, but if her retirement is tardy, or if she fails to retire and is subsequently disqualified, she shall score four points more than the number of yachts entitled to **start** in the race.

(d) A yacht which infringes a rule shortly before or when **finishing** shall be considered to have retired with reasonable promptness if she notifies the Race Committee of her retirement as soon as is reasonably practicable.

(e) A yacht which does not **finish** for a reason other than an infringement shall score points equal to the number of yachts entitled to **start** in the race, except as provided in (f).

(f) After all the yachts of one team have **finished** or retired, the Race Committee may stop the race and allot to each yacht of the other team which is still **racing** and under way, the points she would have received had she **finished.**

(g) The team with the lowest total point score shall be the winner of the race.

6. **Reports and Declarations**

(a) A yacht which retires shall promptly report that fact and the reason therefor to the Race Committee, and if it resulted from a rule infringement she shall state:

    (i)   when the infringement occurred;

    (ii) which yacht(s), if any, was involved in the infringement; and

    (iii) when she retired.

The sailing instructions may require her to submit within a prescribed time a signed statement covering (i), (ii), and (iii).

(b) The sailing instructions may require a yacht to sign a declaration within a prescribed time in accordance with rule 14, Award of Prizes, Places and Points.

(c) A yacht which fails either:

(i) to report her retirement in accordance with rule 6(*a*) above; or

(ii) to sign such declaration as may be required under rule 6(*b*) above, shall be awarded points on the assumption that she retired tardily owing to a rule infringement.

☆ 7. **The Match and Breaking Ties**

(*a*) When two teams only are competing:

(i) The team winning the greater number of races shall be the winner of the match.

(ii) When there is a tie because each team has won the same number of races it shall be resolved in favor of the winner of the last race.

(*b*) When more than two teams are competing in a series consisting of races each of which is between two teams:

(i) The team winning the greatest number of races shall be the winner of the match.

(ii) When there is a tie because two or more teams have won the same number of races, the winner shall be the team which has beaten the other tied team or teams in the most races, or if still tied, the team with the lowest point score, or if still tied, the team which beat the other in the last race between them.

(*c*) When more than two teams are all competing in each race:

(i) The team with the lowest total point score in all races sailed shall be the winner of the match.

(ii) When there is a tie the winner shall be the team which has beaten the other tied team or teams in the most races, or if still tied, the team which beat the other team or teams in the last race.

(*d*) Notwithstanding the above provisions for breaking ties, a tie shall instead be resolved by a sail-off, if practicable, in which case the time for the sail-off shall be scheduled before the series starts.

ADDENDUM

RULES RECOMMENDED TO APPLY WHEN THE HOME TEAM FURNISHES ALL RACING YACHTS

A. Allotment of Yachts. The home team shall furnish the visiting team with a list of the yachts to be used and of the sail numbers assigned to each yacht for the match. The home team shall divide these yachts into as many equal groups as there are competing teams and these groups shall be drawn for by lot for the first race. The yachts shall then be allotted to the crews by each team, except that a helmsman shall not at any time steer the yacht of which he is normally the helmsman. The groups of yachts shall be exchanged between races so that, as far as possible, each group will be sailed in turn by each team. In a two team match after an even number of races, if either team requests that the yachts be regrouped, the home team shall re-divide them into new groups which shall be drawn for by lot; except that for the final odd race of a two-team match, the visiting team may select the group it wishes to sail.

B. **Allotment of Sails.** If sails as well as yachts are provided by the home team, the sails used by each yacht in the first race shall be used by her throughout the series and the substitution of a spare or extra sail shall not be permitted unless because of damage or for some other valid reason, a change is approved by the Race Committee after notification to both teams.

C. **Group Identification.** One group shall carry no markings. The second group shall carry dark colored strips or pennants, and additional groups shall carry light or differently colored strips or pennants. Strips or pennants should usually be provided by the home team and should be attached to the same conspicuous place on each boat of a group, such as the after end of the main boom or permanent backstay.

D. **Breakdowns.** When a breakdown results in substantial loss, the Race Committee shall decide whether or not it was the fault of the crew. In general, a breakdown caused by defective equipment, or the result of a foul by an opponent shall not be deemed the fault of the crew, and a breakdown caused by careless handling or capsizing shall be. In case of doubt, the doubt shall be resolved in favor of the crew.

E. If the Race Committee decides that the breakdown was not the fault of the crew and that a reasonably competent crew could not have remedied the defect in time to prevent substantial loss, it shall cancel the race or order the race to be resailed, or award the breakdown yacht the number of points she would have received had she finished in the same position in the race she held when she broke down. In case of doubt as to her position when she broke down, the doubt shall be resolved against her.

F. **Spares.** The home team shall be prepared to provide one or more extra yachts and sails to replace any which, in the opinion of the Race Committee, are unfit for use in the remaining races.

APPENDIX 1

Amateur

1. For the purpose of international yacht races in which yachts entering are required to have one or more amateurs on board, and in other races with similar requirements, an amateur is a yachtsman who engages in yacht racing as a pastime as distinguished from a means of obtaining a livelihood. No yachtsman shall lose amateur status by rea-

son of the fact that his livelihood is derived from designing or constructing any boats or parts of boats, or accessories of boats, or sails or from other professions associated with the sea and ships.

2. Any yachtsman whose amateur status is questioned or is in doubt, may apply to the National Authority of the country of his residence for recognition of his amateur status. Any such applicant may be required to provide such particulars and evidence and to pay such fee as the National Authority may prescribe. Recognition may be suspended or cancelled by the National Authority by which it was granted.

3. The permanent committee of the International Yacht Racing Union, or any tribunal nominated by the chairman of that committee, may review the decision of any Authority as to the amateur status of a yachtsman for the purpose of competing in international races.

4. For the purposes of participation in the Olympic Regatta an amateur is required to conform to the eligibility rules of the International Olympic Committee. Information on these eligibility requirements is available from all National Authorities.

APPENDIX 2

"Pumping" Sails, "Ooching" and "Rocking"

"Pumping" consists of frequent rapid trimming of sails with no particular reference to a change in true or apparent wind direction. To promote planing or surfing, rapid trimming of sails need not be considered "pumping".

The purpose of this interpretation of rule 60 is to prevent "fanning" one's boat around the course by flapping the sail similar to a bird's wing in flight. "Pumping" or **frequent,** quickly-repeated trimming and releasing of the mainsail to increase propulsion is not allowed and is not "the natural action of the wind on the sails".

Similarly, frequent, quickly-repeated jibing or roll-tacking in calm and near calm conditions fall into the same category as "pumping".

Where surfing or planing conditions exist, however, rule 60 allows taking advantage of "the natural action of water on the hull" through the **rapid** trimming of sails and adjustment of helm to **promote** (initiate) surfing or planing.

The test is whether or not the conditions are such that by **rapid** trimming of sails a boat could be **started** surfing or planing. A skipper challenged for "pumping" will have to prove, through the performance either of his own boat or of other boats, that surfing or planing conditions existed, and that the **frequency** of his **rapid** trimming was geared to the **irregular** or **cyclical** wave forms rather than to a **regular** rhythmic pattern.

Note that the interpretation refers to "promoting" and not to "maintaining" surfing or planing. Once a boat has started surfing or planing on a particular set of wave forms, from then on she must let the natural action of wind and water propel her without further **rapid** trimming and releasing of the sails.

Rapid trimming when approaching marks or the finishing line or other critical points should be consistent with that which was practiced throughout the leg.

"Ooching", which consists of lunging forward and stopping abruptly, falls in the same category as "pumping".

"Rocking" consists of persistently rolling a yacht from side to side.

APPENDIX 3

Alternative Penalties for Infringement of a Rule of Part IV

Experience indicates that the 720° turns penalty is most satisfactory for small boats in relatively short races and it can be dangerous for large boats and not sufficiently severe in long races. The 20% penalty is relatively mild and is designed to encourage acknowledgement of infringements and willingness to protest when not acknowledged. Graduated penalties assign heavier penalties for more serious infringements. All three systems keep yachts racing.

Any one of the three following alternatives to disqualification may be used by including in the sailing instructions a provision such as the following (or if preferred the selected penalty may be quoted in full):—

The 720° turns penalty (or the percentage penalty or graduated penalties) as provided in Appendix 3 of the yacht racing rules will apply instead of disqualification, for infringement of a rule of Part IV.

720° Turns

A yacht which acknowledges infringing a rule of Part IV may exonerate herself by making two full 360° turns (720°) subject to the following provisions:

1. The yacht infringed against shall notify the infringing yacht at the first reasonable opportunity by hail and by showing a protest flag. (The first reasonable opportunity for a hail is usually immediately.)

2. Upon such notification, the yacht acknowledging fault shall immediately start to get well clear of other yachts and while on the same leg of the course she shall hail adjacent yachts of her intention and then make her turns. While so doing, she shall keep clear of all other yachts until she has completed her turns and is on a **proper course** to the next **mark.**

66

3. For the purpose of applying this penalty, "a leg of the course" shall be deemed terminated when two boat lengths from the **mark** ending that leg, and the next leg shall be deemed to commence at this point except for the final leg which is terminated when a yacht is no longer **racing.**

4. The turns may be made in either direction but both in the same direction.

5. When the infringement occurs before the starting signal, the infringing yacht shall make her turns after the starting signal and before **starting.**

6. When an infringement occurs at the finishing line, the infringing yacht shall make her turns on the last leg of the course before being officially finished.

7. If neither yacht acknowledges fault, a protest may be lodged in accordance with rule 68, Protests, and the sailing instructions.

8. An infringing yacht shall report her infringement and the resulting action taken by her to the Race Committee, together with such other information as may be required by the sailing instructions.

9. Failure to observe the above requirements will render a yacht which has infringed a rule of Part IV liable to disqualification or other penalty.

10. An infringing yacht involved in a collision which results in serious damage to either yacht shall be liable to disqualification.

Percentage

1. A yacht which acknowledges infringing a rule of Part IV shall be penalized by receiving the score for the place worse than her actual finishing position by 20% to the nearest whole number of the number of starters in that race, except that the penalty shall be at least three places and except further that in no case will she receive a score for a position worse than one more than the number of starters. (Examples: An infringing yacht which finishes eighth in a start of nineteen yachts will receive the score for twelfth place (19 x 0.2=3.8 or 4); an infringing yacht which finishes thirteenth in a start of fourteen yachts will receive the score for fifteenth place.)

(*a*) A yacht infringing a rule in more than one incident shall receive a 20% penalty for each incident.

(*b*) The imposition of a 20% penalty on a yacht shall not affect the score of other yachts. (Thus two yachts may receive the same score.)

2. The yacht infringed against shall notify the infringing yacht at the first reasonable opportunity by hail and by showing a protest flag. (The first reasonable opportunity for a hail is usually immediately.)

3. A yacht which acknowledges infringing a rule of Part IV shall at the first reasonable opportunity show International Code flag "I",

or such other signal as the sailing instructions may specify, keep it flying until she has finished and report the infringement to the Race Committee.

4. A yacht which fails to acknowledge an infringement as provided in paragraph 3 and which, after a protest and hearing, is found to have infringed a rule of Part IV, shall be penalized 30% or at least five places instead of 20%.

5. A yacht which has shown International Code flag "I" during a race and has not reported the infringement to the Race Committee shall be liable to the 30% penalty of paragraph 4 without a hearing except on the two points of having shown the flag and having reported the infringement to the Race Committee.

6. An infringing yacht involved in a collision which results in serious damage to either yacht shall be liable to disqualification.

Graduated

1. A yacht that infringes a Rule of NAYRU's Part IV (Sailing Rules When Yachts Meet) may continue racing and complete the course, after which she shall have her Finishing Place in that race adjusted by one of the following Penalty Percents; plus the extra 10% of Section 4, when applicable.

2. The following infringements are assigned Specific Penalty Percents, taking precedence over the General Penalty Percents of Section 3:

    a. Infringement of Rule 42.3, the "anti-bargaining" rule   40%
    b. Infringement of Rule 42.2(a), "forcing an overlap" at a Mark or Obstruction 40%
    c. Infringement of Rule 36 (port-tack yacht keep clear) if, while heading for the line to start or on any windward leg, the starboard-tack yacht is forced to tack to avoid collision; or because of collision 40%
    d. Infringement of Rule 44, Yachts Returning to Start; or infringement when the yachts are on different legs of the course 40%
    e. Touching a mark, if a rerounding was not properly performed in accordance with Rule 52.2; or if that section is suspended by the Sailing Instructions. 20%
    f. If the innocent yacht is recorded as DNS or DNF because of collision damage; or because of collision injury to personnel 100%

3. Other than the Penalty Percents specified above in Section 2 and in Section 4 below, the following General Penalty Percents shall apply for infringements of Part IV. The one fact to be determined is whether or not the innocent yacht lost position to the infringing yacht. Position is deemed lost if the infringing yacht crosses ahead; or if she tacks or jibes too close; or if she terminates the overlap in any way

other than by dropping clear astern. No position is deemed lost if an overlapping infringing yacht terminates the overlap by dropping clear astern; or if the infringement occurs before the innocent yacht heads for the line to start.

 a. Position lost to the infringing yacht 40%
 b. No position lost to the infringing yacht 20%

 4. If an infringing yacht acknowledges her fault by a reasonably prompt hail (such as "my fault" or words to that effect) and by showing International Code Flag "I" (or such other signal as the Sailing Instructions may specify), the applicable Penalty Percent of Section 2 or 3 shall be used. If fault is NOT so acknowledged, but is later admitted or decided by a protest hearing, then an extra 10% shall be added. The specified signal shall be kept flying by the infringing yacht until she has finished and reported her infringement to the Race Committee.

 5. Infringement of a Rule of NAYRU's Part III (General Requirements) or Part V (Other Sailing Rules) may, at the discretion of the Race Committee, be penalized 20% instead of the traditional 100%, provided the infringement did not threaten the safety of any craft or person; or augment the infringing yacht's speed; or otherwise improve either her position anywhere in the race or her time for completing the course.

 6. If there is doubt as to which Penalty Percent to apply, the more severe penalty shall be chosen.

 7. The Penalty Percent for an infringement shall be applied against the number of places obtained by subtracting the infringing yacht's Finishing Place from the place for DSQ (one place worse than the number of "Starters" in that race).

 8. In calculating the number of Penalty Places: (*a*) the minimum penalty shall be one place; (*b*) decimal parts of places shall be rounded off to the nearest whole number; (*c*) .5 shall be counted as a full Penalty Place.

 9. The resulting whole number is the number of Penalty Places to be added to the infringing yacht's Finishing Place, thus obtaining her Adjusted Finish.

 10. A yacht infringing during more than one incident in the same race shall have her most-severe Penalty Percent from each incident totalled (but not exceeding 100%) before calculation of her Penalty Places and Adjusted Finish.

 11. When penalties are less than 100%, the assignment of Adjusted Finishes shall not affect the Finishing Places of other yachts. (Thus two yachts may receive the same score in a race when one's Adjusted Finish is the same as another's Finishing Place.)

 12. If an infringement occurs between yachts of different fleets, the protest rules and/or penalties of the infringing yacht's fleet shall govern.

An example of the Adjusted-Finish calculation:

In a 20-boat race, the 2nd-place finisher committed an infringement that did not cause the innocent yacht to lose position. When the 20% penalty was applied against the 19 places obtained by subtracting 2nd from 21st (for DSQ), the infringing yacht was scored as if finishing in 6th place. The calculation: 20% of 19 = .2 x 19 = 3.8 = 4 Penalty Places which, when added to 2nd place, gave the infringing yacht an Adjusted Finish of 6th place.

APPENDIX 4

Limitation of Starters in International Races and Principal National Events

In order to provide good conditions and fair competition, the Permanent Committee of the I.Y.R.U. urges all Race Committees and sponsoring organizations that are responsible for arranging international races and principal national events to observe one of the following procedures laid down in *The Organisation of Principal Events* (1973 I.Y.R.U. year book, pages 112-113) regarding the limitation of the number of starters:

(*a*) The number of starters for an international race or principal national event should be limited to thirty boats.

(*b*) Should the number of entries be higher, two cases may occur: either the number in excess is less or more than twenty per cent of the number established above.

Supposing this number to have been established as thirty, if the excess is lower than twenty per cent, a maximum number of thirty-six boats will be allowed to start. If the excess is higher than twenty per cent, competitors will be divided into heats, each heat having approximately the same number of competitors.

(*c*) In the event of a series with an excessive number of entries, the boats assembled will sail elimination races: afterwards a fixed proportion of the best boats ranked will enter the final series (to consist of a minimum of four races), with the scoring to start again at the beginning of the final series.

(*d*) Two examples of elimination series are given for possible guidance, assuming in each case there are ninety entries:

Example (i). The ninety boats are divided into three heats of thirty boats each. Each heat sails the three races without any change in the distribution of the boats. The ten boats best placed in each heat enter the final series, the other boats being eliminated. Scoring in the finals is based solely on the final races, and points for the preliminary races are not taken into consideration.

Example (ii). Obviously, should the entries be ninety, there will be three heats of thirty boats each, should they be fifty, there will be two heats of twenty-five boats each.

Taking the number as ninety, divide the ninety boats in nine groups of ten each lettered A, B, C, D, E, F, G, H, I.

In the first race there will be three heats:–

First heat	A	B	C
Second heat	D	E	F
Third heat	G	H	I

In the second race the heats will be:–

First heat	A	D	G
Second heat	B	E	H
Third heat	C	F	I

In the third race the heats will be:–

First heat	A	E	I
Second heat	C	F	G
Third heat	H	D	B

This does not result in every boat racing against every other boat, but it gets the greatest possible mix. Upon completion of the three elimination races, the thirty boats with the best point scores enter the final races. In case of ties for thirtieth all boats so tied will enter the final races. Those boats not qualifying for the final races will sail in a secondary series.

APPENDIX 5

Authority and Responsibility of Race Committee and Jury for Rule Enforcement

The authority of the Race Committee and Jury for rule enforcement is well and clearly established in the rules as follows:

Rule 1.1: "All races shall be arranged, conducted and judged by a Race Committee under the direction of the sponsoring organization, except as may be provided under rule 1.2."

Rule 1.2: "For a special regatta or series, the sponsoring organization may provide for a Jury or judges to hear and decide protests and to have supervision over the conduct of the races, in which case the Race Committee shall be subject to the direction of the Jury or judges to the extent provided by the sponsoring organization."

Rule 1.3: "All yachts entered or **racing** shall be subject to the direction and control of the Race Committee . . ."

Ways and means of exercising enforcement are provided in Part VI, rules 69 to 73 inclusive, which set up procedures for conducting hearings regarding alleged or apparent infringements, for notifying yachts of such charges and for penalizing infringers. In particular is to be noted rule 73 which reads in part:

71

Rule 73.1(*a*): "A yacht which fails either to **start** or to **finish** may be disqualified without protest or hearing, after the conclusion of the race . . ."

Rule 73.2: "When the Race Committee:

(*a*) sees an apparent infringement . . .

(*b*) has reasonable grounds for believing that an infringement has resulted in serious damage, or

(*c*) receives a report . . . from a witness . . . not an interested party . . . alleging an infringement,

it may notify such yacht thereof . . . and act thereon . . . as if it had been a protest made by a competitor."

From the quotations and references above, it is clear that the rules provide ample authority to the Race Committee and Jury to enforce the rules and in fact authority beyond that which is ordinarily exercised, while at the same time the rules contain very little which is explicitly directed towards the responsibility which these bodies should assume beyond the deciding of protests. To repeat: "All races shall be judged by a Race Committee" and "All yachts **racing** shall be subject to the direction and control of the Race Committee" give the Race Committee full authority to act on apparent infringements, subject only to the limitations of the procedures established by the rules. It is probably wise that the rules are silent as to the extent to which the Race Committee is required to initiate proceedings when apparent infringements come to its attention, just as they permit but do not require competitors to lodge protests, but it would seem clear from rule 73.2 that the Race Committee is expected to initiate proceedings in the exercise of its authority. To what extent should it do so?

It is well accepted that the seriousness of infringements varies greatly, even while recognizing that an infringement, no matter how minor, is still an infringement. An infringement can be so slight that it has no effect whatever on the speed, course or relative position of either yacht; it can be so serious that it results in a collision, disabling both yachts; and it can by almost imperceptible steps be anything between these two extremes. Very few yachtsmen feel inclined to protest a slight infringement that has no bearing whatever on the result of a race. On the other hand, an infringement which involves the risk of serious damage—even if no contact actually occurs—should be, but is not always, protested; nor does the infringing yacht always retire. The same can be said of many other infringements which, while less serious, still result in places gained and lost. It therefore is in the best interests of yacht racing that such infringements should result in the retirement, disqualification or otherwise penalizing of the infringing yacht, and that yachtsmen themselves should be encouraged to see that this occurs.

One way to bring about greater observance of the rules is for Race Committees to institute more proceedings under rule 73.2. Why has there grown up a tendency on the part of Race Committees not to do so? There are several reasons. For one thing, the Race Committee feels that it is the prerogative and therefore, the function of competitors to lodge protests. For another, there is a natural disinclination to increase the burden of holding protest hearings. For still another, it is felt that the Race Committee sees only a small part of the race and why therefore should it call someone to account for something which happens nearby when there may be many other incidents which it cannot see at all? In some instances, too, if feels that since it is to sit in judgement on a case, it should not also be in the position of a prosecutor. But this overlooks the fact that the Race Committee is an umpire as well as a judge. When a protest is lodged and a hearing held on an incident not seen by the Race Committee, it performs a judging function in determining the facts and interpreting the rules to arrive at a decision. But when it sees what it believes to be a clear infringement and no protest results, the rules certainly give it authority and somewhat more than an implied responsibility—assuming the infringement is serious and not trivial, and here of course judgement must be used—to take the prescribed steps of rule enforcement. It is, to be sure, recognized that, unlike other sports in which the umpire calls infringements when and as he sees them, the Race Committee is required to hold a hearing and give the alleged infringer an opportunity to tell his story, but this difference is a difference in procedure, not in function or responsibility.

The philosophy that in matters of infringements the Race Committee's function is solely that of judging is sometimes put forward more strongly for the Jury, when there is one, than for the Race Committee itself, but this distinction is not supported by the rules. Rule 1.1 says that "all races shall be conducted and judged by a Race Committee." Rule 1.2 says the same thing a little differently, in that a Jury is appointed "to hear and decide protests and to have supervision over the conduct of the races." Surely the conduct and judging of races includes the right—and the responsibility—to initiate action to enforce the rules. Juries and Race Committees are expected to be impartial, but partiality is not bringing to a hearing a personal observation of an incident but a desire to favor or penalize one or another competitor. The reason Juries are selected for important regattas is not to set up the judging function apart from other functions of the Race Committee, but to provide as impartial and experienced umpires as possible.

Fully recognizing some of the dangers involved, such as becoming overzealous, Race Committees and Juries should institute hearings under rule 73.2 when there occurs what appears to be a clear-cut and significant rule infringement not protested by a competitor.

73

APPENDIX 6

A Prescription to Racing Rule 68.4,
Protests Involving Measurement and Rating Certificates

General

A protest under the provisions of Rule 68.4 and involving a certificate issued by NAYRU (IOR or CCA Measurement Rules) should be referred to the NAYRU Offshore Administrative Committee by mailing a copy of the protest and the protested yacht's certificate to the NAYRU Offshore Executive Director. The Offshore Administrative Committee will make its decision, and may consult with the NAYRU, ORC, or CCA Technical Committees.

Note that Rule 68.4 *requires* the Race Committee to refer such protests to "an authority qualified to decide . . ." and to "be governed by the determination of such authority." The NAYRU Offshore Administrative Committee is the "qualified authority" for questions regarding the IOR or CCA Rules.

The committee of a one-design class which has the responsibility for measurement and the issuing of measurement certificates is the "qualified authority" for questions regarding that class's measurement rules.

Administrative Protests

In addition to the provisions of Rule 68.4, Administrative Protests concerning Measurement Rules administered by NAYRU's Offshore Administrative Committee may be filed directly with the Committee in care of the Offshore Executive Director.

The Administrative Protest procedure has been established to permit protests of rating certificates at any time after issuance, without regard to whether or not the yacht was *racing*.

Any person or organization which has a sufficiently valid interest in a yacht's certificate may use the Administrative Protest procedure, as follows:

1. The protest must be in writing and shall be dated and signed by the protestor.
2. The protest must include a detailed description of the alleged defect(s) and a full statement supporting a valid interest on the part of the protestor such as owner of a yacht holding a rating certificate, a certified measurer, a Race Committee sponsoring offshore racing.
3. The protest must be accompanied by a copy of the certificate being protested and the current address and telephone number of the owner of the protested yacht.
4. The protest must include a statement of the issue the protestor wishes to have resolved, identification of appropriate Measurement Rules, and other appropriate evidence.
5. A copy of the Administrative Protest and supporting materi-

als must be mailed to the owner of the protested yacht by the protestor.

6. The protest must be accompanied by the Administrative Protest filing fee of $25.

7. The owner of a protested yacht should file a reply with the Offshore Executive Director, in writing, as soon as possible.

8. The Offshore Executive Director will circulate copies of the protest and reply to the members of the Offshore Administrative Committee. The Administrative Committee shall make its decision based on the available evidence and additional evidence it may obtain, and it may order remeasurement of the yacht in whole or part.

9. The Administrative Committee may consult with or refer the matter to the appropriate rule making authority.

10. If the owner of the protested yacht elects to concede the protest or refuses to cooperate in providing for remeasurement, the Executive Director shall invalidate the protested yacht's certificate and so advise all concerned, including the local organization under which the yacht normally races.

11. The decision of the Administrative Committee shall be made as promptly as circumstances permit and shall be communicated in writing to the protestor and protestee.

12. The Administrative Committee shall determine which party will pay and the amount of costs of determining the protest using guidelines as follows:

a) Unless the correct rating of the protested yacht is higher than the protested rating by more than .2 feet or 0.5% (whichever is greater), the protestor will be responsible for the costs. The $25 filing fee will not be counted towards payment of costs.

b) If the correct rating increased by more than .2 feet or 0.5% (whichever is greater), costs will be borne (or shared) by the owner, the measurer(s), or NAYRU, depending upon the determination of responsibility for the defect. The $25 filing fee will be returned to the protestor.

One-design classes may institute a similar procedure with the appropriate class committee or officer taking the place of the Offshore Administrative Committee.

APPENDIX 7

INTERNATIONAL YACHT RACING UNION RULES
BEFORE N.A.Y.R.U. PRESCRIPTIONS

8—Recalls

1.   Unless otherwise prescribed by the National Authority or in the sailing instructions, the Race Committee may allot a recall number or letter to each yacht, in accordance with rule 3.2(*b*)(viii), using yachts' sail numbers or letters when practicable.

18—Entries

Unless otherwise prescribed by the National Authority or by the Race Committee in either the notice or the sailing instructions, entries shall be made in the following form:—

FORM OF ENTRY

To the Secretary. . . . . Club
Please enter the yacht. . . . . .for
the. . . . . race, on the. . . . .
Her distinguishing flag is . . . .
her national letters and distinguishing numbers are. . . . .
her rig is . . . .
the color of her hull is . . . .
and her rating or class is. . . . .
I agree to be bound by the racing rules of the I.Y.R.U., by the pre-
scriptions of the National Authority under which this race is sailed, by
the sailing instructions and by the class rules.
     Name. . . . .
     Address. . . . .
     Telephone No. . . . .
     Club. . . . .
Signed . . . . Date. . . . .
(Owner or owner's representative)
Entrance fee enclosed

25—Sail Numbers, Letters and Emblems

2.   Other yachts shall comply with the rules of their National Authority or class in regard to the allotment, carrying and size of sail numbers, letters and emblems, which rules should, so far as they may be applicable, conform to the above requirements.

28—Flags

A National Authority may prescribe the flag usage which shall be observed by yachts unders its jurisdiction.

72—Disqualification After Protest

4. The question of damages arising from an infringement of any of these rules or the sailing instructions shall be governed by the prescriptions, if any, of the National Authority.

77—Appeals

1. Unless otherwise prescribed by the National Authority which has recognized the sponsoring organization concerned, an appeal against the decision of a Race Committee shall be governed by rules 77, Appeals, and 78, Particulars to be Supplied in Appeals.

2. Unless otherwise prescribed by the National Authority or in the sailing instructions (subject to rule 2(*j*) or 3.2(*b*)(xvii)), a protest which has been decided by the Race Committee shall be referred to the National Authority solely on a question of interpretation of these rules, within such period after the receipt of the Race Committee's decision, as the National Authority may decide:—

> (*a*) when the Race Committee, at its own instance, thinks proper to do so, or
>
> (*b*) when any of the parties involved in the protest makes application for such reference.

This reference shall be accompanied by such deposit as the National Authority may prescribe, payable by the appellant, to be forfeited to the funds of the National Authority in the event of the appeal being dismissed.

3. The National Authority shall have power to uphold or reverse the decision of the Race Committee, and if it is of opinion, from the facts found by the Race Committee, that a yacht involved in a protest has infringed an applicable rule, it shall disqualify her, irrespective of whether the rule or sailing instruction which led to such disqualification was mentioned in the protest.

4. The decision of the National Authority, which shall be final, shall be communicated in writing to all interested parties.

5. (*a*) In the Olympic Regatta and such international regattas as may be specially approved by the I.Y.R.U., the decisions of the Jury or judges shall be final.

> (*b*) Other international Regattas shall be under the jurisdiction of the National Authority of the country in which the Regatta is held, and if satisfied that a competent international Jury has been appointed, it may give consent for the decisions of the Jury to be final.

6. An appeal once lodged with the National Authority shall not be withdrawn.

78—Particulars to be Supplied in Appeals

1.   The reference to the National Authority shall be in writing and shall contain the following particulars, in order, so far as they are applicable:—

(*a*) A copy of the notice of the race and the sailing instructions supplied to the yachts.

(*b*) A copy of the protest, or protests, if any, prepared in accordance with rule 68.3(d), and all other written statements which may have been put in by the parties.

(*c*) The observations of the Race Committee thereon, a full statement of the facts found, its decision and the grounds thereof.

(*d*) An official diagram prepared by the Race Committee in accordance with the facts found by it, showing:—

(i) the course to the next **mark,** or, if close by, the **mark** itself with the required side;

(ii) the direction and force of the wind;

(iii) the set and strength of the current, if any;

(iv) the depth of water, if relevant; and

(v) the positions and courses of all the yachts involved.

(vi) Where possible, yachts should be shown sailing from the bottom of the diagram towards the top.

(*e*) The grounds of the appeal, to be supplied by either:—

(i) the Race Committee under rule 77.2(a); or

(ii) the appellant under rule 77.2(b).

(*f*) Observations, if any, upon the appeal by the Race Committee or any of the parties.

2.   The Race Committee shall notify all parties that an appeal will be lodged and shall invite them to make any observations upon it. Any such observation shall be forwarded with the appeal.

APPENDIX 8

EXCERPTS FROM THE INTERNATIONAL REGULATIONS FOR PREVENTING COLLISIONS AT SEA—1963
(To be replaced in 1976 by new Regulations)

PART B.—LIGHTS AND SHAPES

Rule 5

(b) In addition to the lights prescribed in section (a), a sailing vessel may carry on the top of the foremast two lights in a vertical line one over the other, sufficiently separated so as to be clearly distinguished. The upper light shall be red and the lower light shall be green. Both lights shall be constructed and fixed as prescribed in rule 2(a)(i) and shall be visible at a distance of at least 2 miles. [Note: 2(a)(i) calls for a light "to show an unbroken light over an arc of the horizon of 225° so fixed as to show from right ahead to 2 points abaft the beam on either side."]

Rule 12

Every vessel or seaplane on the water may, if necessary in order to attract attention, in addition to the lights which she is by these rules required to carry, show a flare up light or use a detonating or other efficient sound signal that cannot be mistaken for any signal authorized elsewhere under these rules.

PART D.—STEERING AND SAILING RULES

Preliminary

1. *In obeying and construing these rules, any action taken should be positive, in ample time, and with due regard to the observance of good seamanship.*

2. *Risk of collision can, when circumstances permit, be ascertained by carefully watching the compass bearing of an approaching vessel. If the bearing does not appreciably change, such risk should be deemed to exist.*

4. *Rules 17 to 24 apply only to vessels in sight of one another.*

Rule 17

(a) When two sailing vessels are approaching one another, so as to involve risk of collision, one of them shall keep out of the way of the other as follows:

(i) When each has the wind on a different side, the vessel which has the wind on the port side shall keep out of the way of the other.

(ii) When both have the wind on the same side, the vessel which is to windward shall keep out of the way of the vessel which is to leeward.

(b) For the purposes of this rule the windward side shall be deemed to be the side opposite to that on which the mainsail is carried or, in the case of a square-rigged vessel, the side opposite to that on which the largest fore-and-aft sail is carried.

Rule 20

(a) When a power-driven vessel and a sailing vessel are proceeding in such directions as to involve risk of collision, except as provided for in rules 24 and 26, the power-driven vessel shall keep out of the way of the sailing vessel.

(b) This rule shall not give to a sailing vessel the right to hamper, in a narrow channel, the safe passage of a power-driven vessel which can navigate only inside such channel.

Rule 22

Every vessel which is directed by these rules to keep out of the way of another vessel shall, so far as possible, take positive early action to comply with this obligation, and shall, if the circumstances of the case admit, avoid crossing ahead of the other.

Rule 24

(a) Notwithstanding anything contained in these rules, every vessel overtaking any other shall keep out of the way of the overtaken vessel.

(b) Every vessel coming up with another vessel from any direction more than 22½° (2 points) abaft her beam, i.e., in such a position, with reference to the vessel which she is overtaking, that at night she would be unable to see either of that vessel's sidelights, shall be deemed to be an overtaking vessel; and no subsequent alteration of the bearing between the two vessels shall make the overtaking vessel a crossing vessel within the meaning of these rules, or relieve her of the duty of keeping clear of the overtaken vessel until she is finally past and clear.

(c) If the overtaking vessel cannot determine with certainty whether she is forward of or abaft this direction from the other vessel, she shall assume that she is an overtaking vessel and keep out of the way.

Rule 26

All vessels not engaged in fishing, except vessels to which the provisions of rule 4 apply, shall, when under way, keep out of the way of vessels engaged in fishing.

The International Rules apply to vessels on the high seas. The Inland Rules apply to vessels on inland waters including coastal areas.

Copies of the complete regulations, both International and Inland, may be obtained from the United States Coast Guard.

PROTEST COMMITTEE PROCEDURE
in Outline Form

Rules Concerning Protests—68, 69, 70, 71, 72, 73 and 75.

Preliminaries

1. Note on the protest the time it is received.

2. Determine whether the protest contains the information called for by rule 68.3(d) in sufficient detail to identify the incident and to tell the recipient what the protest is about. If not, ask the protestor to supply the information (rule 68.3 (f)).

3. Inquire whether the protestor flew a protest flag in accordance with rule 68.3(*a*) unless rule 68.3(*b*) applied or the protestor is seeking redress under rule 68.5(*a*) and note his answer on the protest.

4. Inquire whether the protestor tried to inform the yacht(s) protested against (the protestee(s)) that a protest would be lodged (rule 68.3(*c*)) and note his answer on the protest.

5. Unless rule 69 applies, promptly notify the protestee(s).

6. Hold a hearing as soon as possible when the protest conforms to the requirements of rule 68 (see 1, 2, 3 and 4 above). Notify the representative of each yacht involved of the time and place of the hearing (rule 70.1).

The Hearing

1. The representative of each yacht involved in the incident is entitled to be present throughout the hearing. All others, except one witness at a time while testifying, may be excluded (rule 70.1).

2. Read to the meeting the protest and any other written statement there may be about the incident (such as an account of it from the protestee).

3. Have first the protestor and then the protestee(s) give their accounts of the incident. Each may question the other(s). Questions by the Protest Committee, except for clarifying details, are preferably deferred until all accounts have been presented. Models are helpful. Positions before and after the incident itself are often helpful.

4. Invite the protestor and then the protestee to call witnesses. They may be questioned by the protestor and protestees as well as by the Committee.

5. Invite first the protestor and then the protestee to make a final statement of his case, including any application or interpretation of the rules to the incident as he sees it.

Decision

1. The Protest Committee, after dismissing those involved in the incident, should decide what the relevant facts are.

2. The Committee should then apply the rules and reach a decision as to who, if anyone, infringed a rule and what rule was infringed (rule 71).

3. Having reached a decision, it should record both the findings of fact and the decision in writing, recall the protestor and protestee and read to them the decision (rule 71).

4. Any party involved is entitled to a copy of the decision (rule 71), signed by the Chairman of the Protest Committee. A copy should also be filed with the Committee records.

N.B. The Protest Committee referred to above may be the Race Committee, Judges appointed for the event in which the incident occurred or a Protest Committee established by the Race Committee for the express purpose of handling protests.

Standard Protest Forms are available from the N.A.Y.R.U. at $1.50 for sets of 25.

APPLICATION FOR MEMBERSHIP

NAME . . . .

ADDRESS . . . .

. . . . Zip Code . . . .

Enclosed is check payable to . . . .

NAYRU for annual dues for:

* Sustaining Membership	$25.
* Contributing Membership	$15.
Regular Membership	$10.
Yacht Club Membership	$15 or 25 *

Persons under 25 years of age   ($5.)

Please mail the Year Book, News Letters and other data to the address shown above.

(Membership in these categories helps support the Unions)

Please return this form to the

North American Yacht Racing Union

37 West 44th Street

New York, N.Y. 10036

RACE COMMITTEE SIGNALS

See Rule 4

AP—ANSWERING PENNANT, POSTPONEMENT SIGNAL

L—COME WITHIN HAIL OR FOLLOW ME

M—MARK SIGNAL

N—ABANDONMENT SIGNAL

N OVER X—ABANDONMENT AND RE-SAIL SIGNAL

N OVER 1ST REPEATER—CANCELLATION SIGNAL

R—REVERSE COURSE SIGNAL

S—SHORTENED COURSE SIGNAL

1ST REPEATER—GENERAL RECALL SIGNAL

2

Application of Rules

Shields 70 is a victim here of Rule 36, the most basic rule in yacht racing, and must either tack to leeward of her opponent or bear off (as she is doing) to pass astern of the other yacht. (Photo: Stanley Rosenfeld)

Q.1. Which yacht has the right of way, yacht A or yacht B?

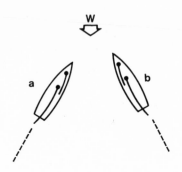

Q.2. Which yacht has the right of way?

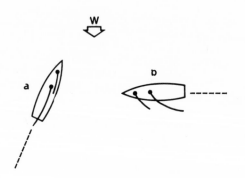

A.1. Yacht B, on starboard tack, has the right of way (Rule 36). Please note that Rule 32, "Avoiding Collisions," also applies to both yachts in this situation.

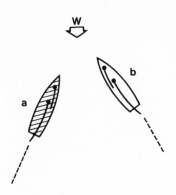

A.2. Yacht B, on starboard tack, has the right of way (Rule 36).

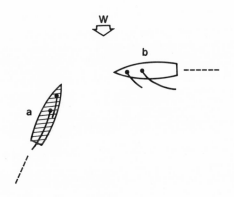

Q.3. Which yacht has the right of way?

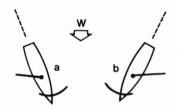

Q.4. Which yacht now has rights?

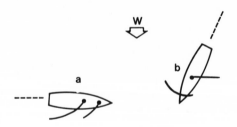

A.3. Yacht B, on starboard tack, has rights over yacht A
(Rule 36).

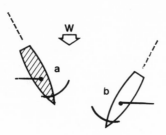

A.4. Once again, yacht B, on starboard tack, has the right of
way.

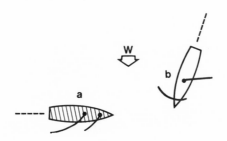

Q.5. Which yacht has the right of way?

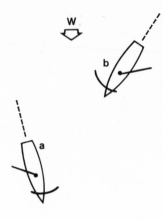

Q.6. Which yacht (or yachts) has the right of way *before* the starting signal?

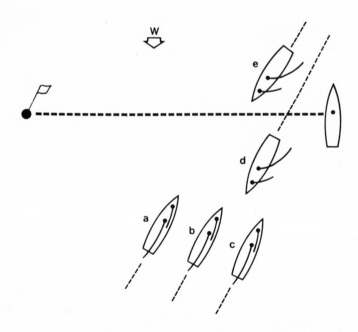

A.5. Yacht B, on starboard tack, again has right of way.

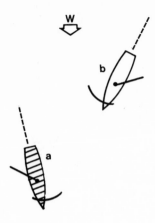

A.6. Yachts D and E, being on starboard tack, have the right of way over yachts A, B, and C (Rule 36).

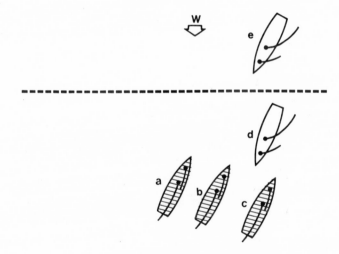

Q.7. Which of these yachts has the right of way *after* the starting signal?

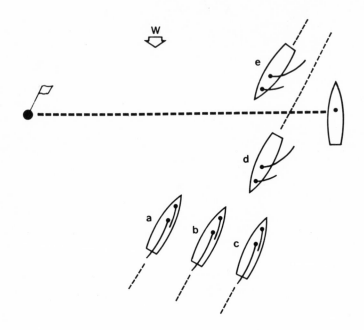

A.7. Yacht D, on starboard tack, and on the correct side of the starting line, has the right of way over yachts A, B, and C. Yacht E, since she is on the wrong side of the line at the starting signal, has no rights at all. She must keep clear of all other yachts, even those on port tack, until she has crossed to the proper side of the starting line. When she crosses, and suddenly acquires rights over yachts A, B, and C, she must still give them "ample room and opportunity to keep clear." See Rule 44.1(b).

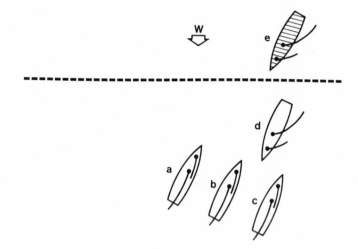

Q.8. Yacht B has begun luffing* yacht A. Can yacht B continue her luff beyond position two?

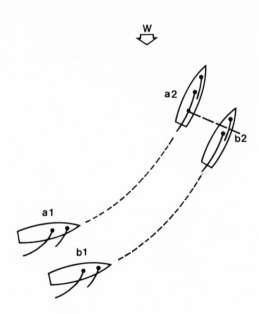

* A yacht "luffs" her opponent when, from a leeward position, she forces her opponent either head-to-wind, or to a higher angle of sail than when the luffing maneuver was inaugurated. Remember when luffing that different sizes and types of racing sailboats will react very differently under certain conditions. A narrow, heavy, deep-keel hull (like an International One-design or a Shields) develops considerable momentum, even in light breezes, and will coast, or "carry" head to wind for a considerable distance. Light, planing sailboats (like the 505 or the *Flying Dutchman*) develop relatively little momentum, and will slow down and even stop very quickly if a luffing maneuver is carried too far. Large, cruising yachts, preparing to start a long ocean race, especially in very heavy wind and sea conditions, must use moderation in luffing competitors, particularly in crowded starting areas.

Throughout this book be aware that the answers are designed to apply to medium-sized yachts racing under average conditions, and guide yourself accordingly.

A.8. If the helmsman of yacht A, in sighting abeam from his normal sailing position, is forward of the mast of yacht B, he can call "Mast abeam" to the helmsman of yacht B. At this point yacht B must immediately alter course so as to return to her proper course to the next mark (Rule 38.1 and 38.3).

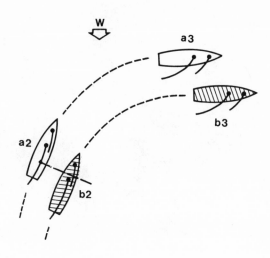

Within two boat-lengths of the mark, International One-Design 9, though ahead, appears to be overlapped by the trailing yacht and must leave room at the mark. Rule 42.1. (Photo: Roger Smith, Bermuda News Bureau)

OPPOSITE, TOP: *"L-24," the trailing 5.5-meter yacht, has no overlap in this situation and must keep clear of the yacht ahead. Rule 37.2.* (Photo: Howey Caufman)

OPPOSITE, BOTTOM: *A tricky situation at the windward mark during the 1972 Olympic Trials. International Tempest US 225, on starboard tack, has started to bear off to round (note wind sock atop mark) and has right-of-way (Rule 36). But 225 must be careful not to obstruct US 1 in his efforts to keep clear of 225 (Rule 34). (Photo: Bob Lindgren)*

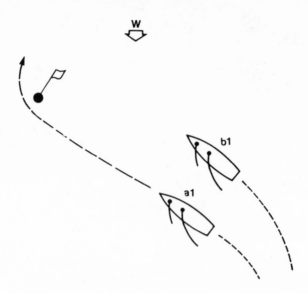

Q.9. May yacht B bear off and converge with yacht A with the intention of blanketing her? (Assume that yacht B is approximately five boat lengths from the turning mark.)

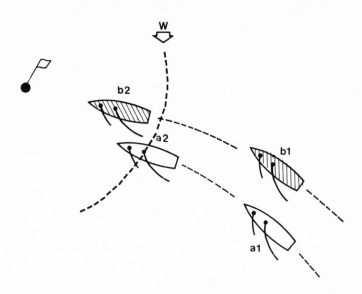

A.9. No, yacht B may not bear off because, in doing so, she would foul yacht A, who has rights (Rule 37.1). However, as soon as the leading yacht, yacht B in this case, reaches the two-boat-length circle, she can claim an inside overlap (Rule 42.1(a)).

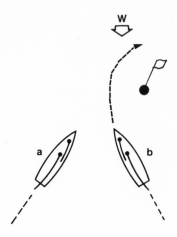

Q.10. In the above situation who has the right of way, yacht A or yacht B?

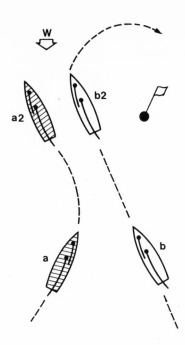

A.10. Yacht B, on starboard tack, has the right of way. Yacht A must change course to avoid B by tacking, or by bearing off astern of yacht B. (*Note:* Yacht B is under no obligation to tack as soon as she has passed the turning mark. She can continue on starboard tack and carry yacht A as far as she likes. See Rule 36.)

On the other hand, A2 has luffing rights over B2, and could luff B head to wind in an effort to encourage her to tack (Rule 38.1, 38.2).

Q.11. Who has the right of way in this situation?

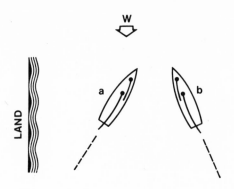

Q.12. May yacht A bear off below her proper course to prevent yacht B from passing to leeward?

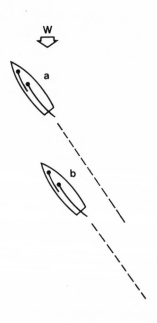

A.11. Yacht B has the right of way since she is on starboard tack. Yacht A will have to either tack or go under yacht B's stern. If she *does* tack, yacht A may fall under Rule 43, "Close-Hauled, Hailing for Room to Tack at Obstructions."

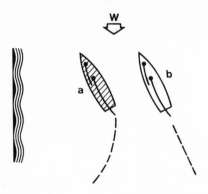

A.12. Since both yachts are sailing hard on the wind, and not on a free leg, Rule 39, "Sailing Below a Proper Course"— would *not* apply in this case. Yacht A can bear off so as to hinder yacht B's overtaking maneuver. However, once an overlap has been established between the two yachts, yacht A would be governed by Rule 37.1, "A windward yacht shall keep clear of a leeward yacht."

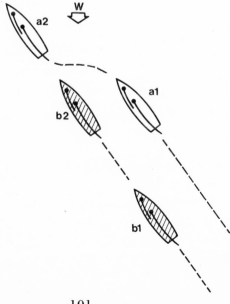

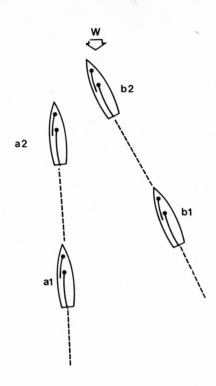

Q.13 Does yacht A, in position A2, have luffing rights over yacht B in position B2?

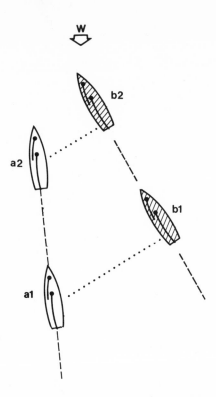

A.13. Yes, yacht A2 has luffing rights over yacht B2. The overlap which A1 established on B1 was not established from behind, but from abeam of B1 at a two-boat-length distance. At no time, starting from the beginning of the overlap, was the helmsman of yacht B, in his normal sailing position, forward of the mainmast of yacht A. In both positions B1 and B2 the helmsman of yacht B is *still* not forward of the mainmast on yacht A. Refer to rule 38.1 and 38.2 "Right of Way Yacht Luffing after Starting."

Q.14. Is yacht B allowed to bear down, as shown, on yacht A?

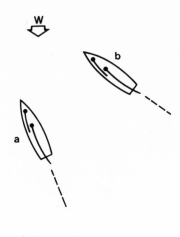

Q.15. May yacht A bear away, or luff at her leisure?

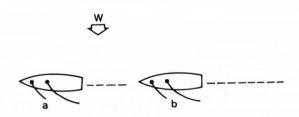

A.14. Yes. Yacht B1 can converge on yacht A1, as shown, until the yachts are in the approximate positions of A2 and B2. B2 cannot interfere with A2 and cannot force her to change course (Rule 37.1 of the Fundamental Rules). In the case shown above, yacht B2 can be luffed by yacht A2, however, and until B2 has rights to call "Mast abeam" she should stay clear of yacht A2.

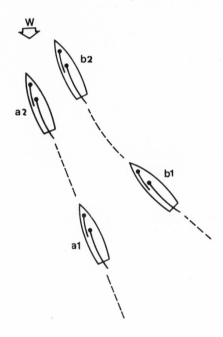

A.15. Yes, yacht A may maneuver as she pleases with no regard to yacht B. However, if yacht B were sailing a course obviously intending to pass yacht A to leeward, yacht A would not be able to sail below her proper course. See Rule 39, "Sailing Below a Proper Course." If yacht B were to establish an overlap to leeward from clear astern on yacht A then yacht A would have further reason to keep clear (Rule 37.1, Fundamental Rules).

A tricky situation for these Star Class yachts at the finish of the seventh race during the 1972 Olympics. KA must keep clear of G 5663, by either tacking immediately, or bearing off under G 5663's stern. (KA eventually went on to win the gold medal.) (Photo: K. Hashimoto)

The windward mark draws a crowd of Stars during the 1971 World Championships in Seattle. 5509 is in a precarious position; she must tack immediately to avoid fouling the starboard-tack yachts, and hope to lay the mark. (Photo: Roy Montgomery)

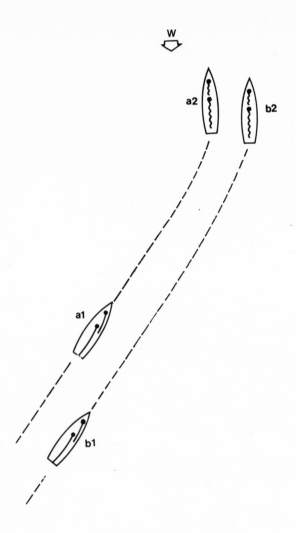

Q.16. May yacht B1 luff yacht A1 as shown in positions B2 and A2?

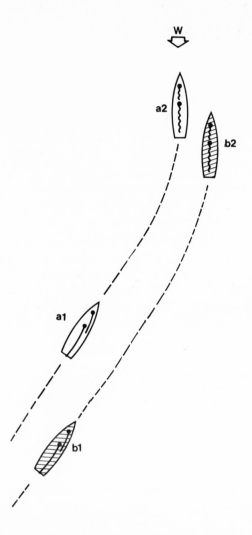

A.16. No. Since yacht B1 established her overlap from clear astern, she has no luffing rights over yacht A2 so long as that overlap continues (Rule 38.1).

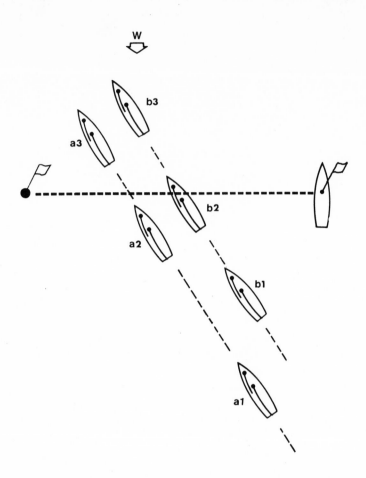

Q.17. Does yacht A in position A3 have luffing rights on yacht B in position B3?

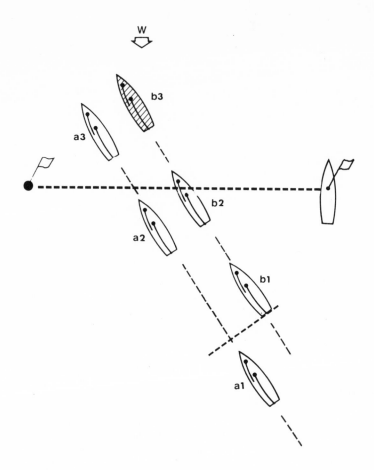

A.17. Yes, even though yacht A originally established her overlap to leeward and from clear astern of yacht B. Rule 38.2 clearly states that when an overlap exists between two yachts, and the leading yacht has crossed the starting line, a new overlap begins at that time. From the instant yacht B at position B2 crossed the starting line, yacht B's helmsman was never ahead of the mainmast position on yacht A, so yacht B can be luffed by yacht A.

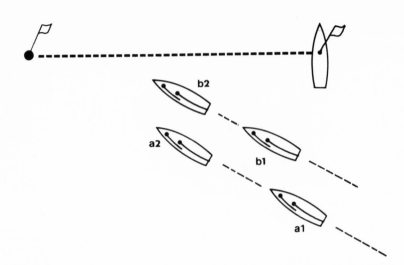

Q.18. The starting gun has not yet fired. Yachts A and B are both sailing on starboard tack, but not hard on the wind. Does yacht A have luffing rights over yacht B at position 2?

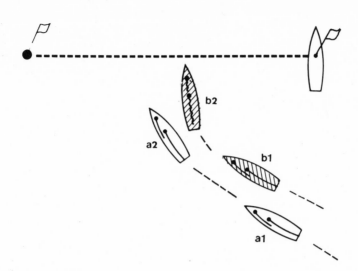

A.18. Yes. Yacht A can sail up to a course hard on the wind (or close-hauled) and force B to change her course in whatever way necessary to avoid yacht A. Prior to the starting signal, this must be done slowly, and in such a way as to give yacht B sufficient room and opportunity to keep clear (Rule 40).

If yacht A continues to pass yacht B so that the helmsman of yacht B, in sighting abeam from his normal position, is now abaft the mainmast position on yacht A, yacht A may luff yacht B head to wind. All of this is possible despite the fact that yacht A established her overlap from clear astern and to leeward.

Q.19. May yacht B tack?

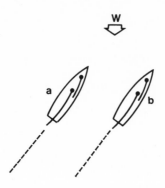

Q.20. Which yacht has the right of way in this situation?

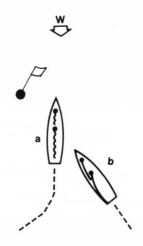

A.19. No, yacht B may not tack. Yacht A can carry her as far as she desires. This situation is covered in Rule 41.1, "Tacking or Jibing." An exception may exist if both yachts are sailing toward an obstruction, but this will be covered by a later rule.

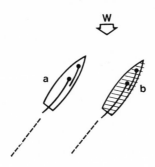

A.20. Yacht B, on starboard tack, has the right of way. Rule 41.1 "Tacking or Jibing" does not apply in this case, as the reader might expect. Technically, yacht A is still on port tack, since she is merely head to wind, and has not yet begun her tack (see definition of "tacking"). Therefore, Rule 36 applies.

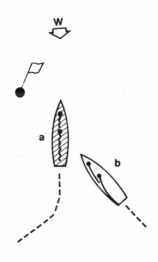

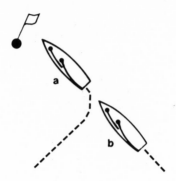

Q.21. In this situation has yacht A fouled yacht B?

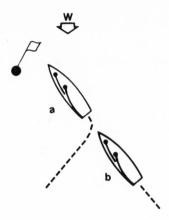

A.21. Yacht A has arrived at the mark slightly ahead of yacht B and has tacked ahead of B. If yacht A has been able to complete her tack before B is forced to change her course in order to avoid a collision, then A is safe (Rule 41.1).

To complete her tack, A needs merely to turn to a close-hauled course. For as the rule states, she is tacking from the moment she is beyond head-to-wind (in the turn) until she bears away to a close-hauled course. Yacht A's sails may be luffing slightly or fully and she may have little or no headway, yet she will be deemed to have completed her tack.

Yacht A, however, is the burdened vessel in this maneuver (see Rule 41.3). In a close situation, where there is a question in the Protest Committee's mind as to what the facts actually were, A must have a strong case to avoid disqualification.

Q.22. Who has the right of way in this windward mark situation?

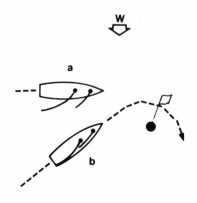

Q.23. Which yacht has rights at this windward mark?

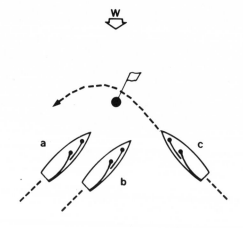

A.22. Yacht B, since she has an inside overlap, has rights at this mark (Rule 42.1(a)(i)).

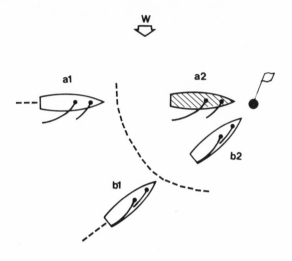

A.23. Again, yacht C on starboard tack has rights over yachts A and B. Yachts A or B would be allowed to tack to leeward of yacht C if they could do so in accordance with Fundamental Rule 36, "Opposite Tack," and Rule 41, "Tacking or Jibing." In this illustration, however, there is not enough room for either one to tack, so they must either bear off astern of yacht C or luff head to wind and go to the other side of the mark. In the illustration, yacht B2 is bearing off astern of yacht C, and will be able to round well ahead of yacht A2.

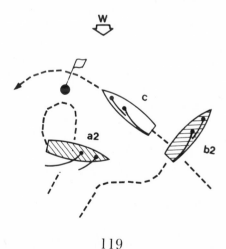

Q.24. Which yacht has rights over the others at this turning mark?

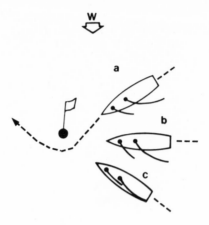

Q.25. May yacht A luff her opponent before reaching the mark?

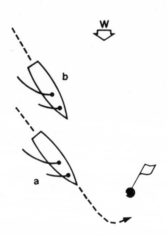

A.24. It appears that yacht A in this situation must be given room to round, but only if she had established her inside overlap on yachts B and C at the time the leading yacht reached the two-boat-length line. See Rule 42.1(a)(i).

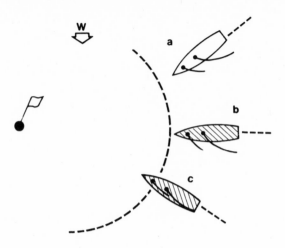

A.25. No she cannot. An outside leeward yacht with luffing rights may luff an inside yacht and carry her to windward of a turning mark provided that (1) she hails to that effect, (2) begins to luff before she is within two boat lengths of the mark, and (3) *she also* passes to windward of the mark. In the illustrations shown, yacht A did not begin to luff before she was two boat lengths from the mark, so she cannot luff yacht B (Rule 42.1(a)(i)).

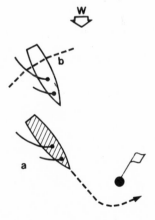

Q.26. Is yacht A under any obligation to give room to yacht B in this situation?

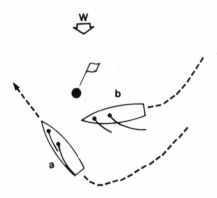

Q.27. May yacht A in position A2 call for room to round the mark?

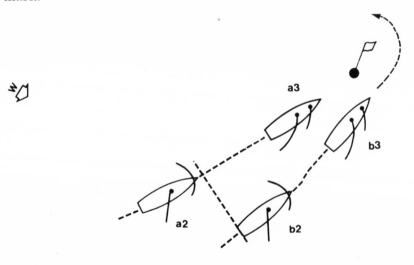

A.26. It all depends on whether or not yacht B had established an inside overlap at the time yacht A's bow crossed the two-boat-length line. (See Rule 42.2(a)). We have assumed that in this situation yacht B did not establish her overlap in time and is therefore the burdened vessel.

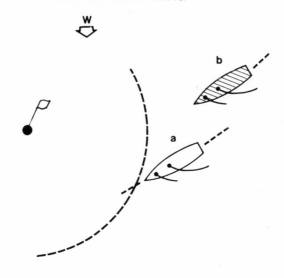

A.27. No. Yacht A does not have rights at the mark. At the time the two-boat-length line was reached, yacht A did not have an inside overlap over yacht B. Rules 42.1(a)(i) and 42.2(a) apply.

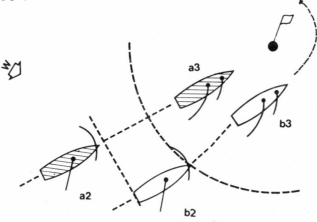

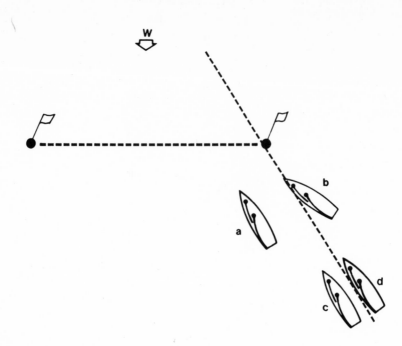

Q.28. May yachts B and D claim room to pass to leeward of the starting mark either before or after the starting signal?

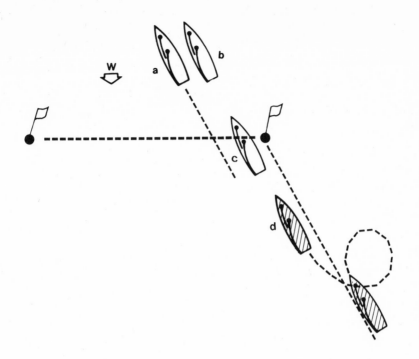

A.28. No. Neither yacht B nor yacht D has rights in this situation. Before the starting signal yacht A could have luffed yacht B to prevent her from crossing the starting line. However, once the starting signal is given, yacht A cannot sail above close-hauled, or above the first mark, and B will be able to cross the line to leeward of the starting mark, since A has left enough room.

In the case of yacht D, there is no way she can gain room to pass to leeward of the starting mark. She must kill speed either by luffing head to wind, by slacking her sheets, or by making a 360-degree turn (as indicated in the diagram) so that she can fall behind yacht C and cross the line. See rule 42.3.

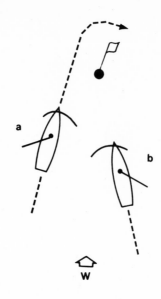

Q.29. Can yacht B call for room at the leeward mark?

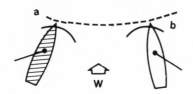

A.29. It would appear that at the time A's bow crossed the two-boat-length line, B had an inside overlap. In this situation, B *does* have rights to room at the mark. See Rules 42.1(a)(i) and 42.2(a).

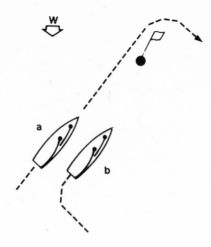

Q.30. In the above situation, does yacht B have the right to
claim an inside overlap at the turning mark? And does B have
luffing rights?

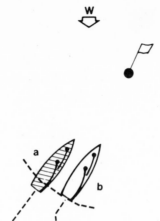

A.30. Yes, yacht B has tacked inside the two-boat-length circle and can demand room from yacht A to round the mark (Rule 42.2(b) applies). Yacht B in this situation also has luffing rights over yacht A, since her tack has started a new overlap situation between the two yachts. Rules 38.1 and 38.2 apply in the luffing situation.

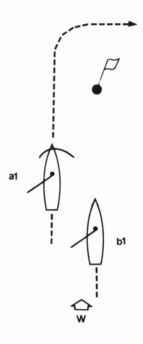

Q.31. Yacht B takes its spinnaker down at position 1 while yacht A continues to carry hers. Subsequently, yacht B loses her overlap on yacht A before reaching the mark. Does yacht B still have inside rights at the mark?

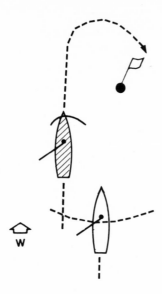

A.31. Yacht B retains her right to an inside position at the turning mark since she *did* have an overlap when yacht A's bow crossed the two-boat-length line. The fact that she subsequently lost the overlap does not mean that she lost her rights to an inside rounding. (Rule 42.2(e)(i)).

Q.32. Does yacht A in this situation have the right to force B to change course?

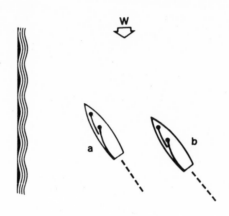

Q.33. Yacht A on port tack can lay the next mark and must round it to starboard. Yacht B, however, cannot tack because she is too close to A (Rule 41.1). Although she has luffing rights, yacht B does not feel she can luff yacht A sufficiently to enable her to round the mark, so she hails yacht A for room to tack. What must yacht A do?

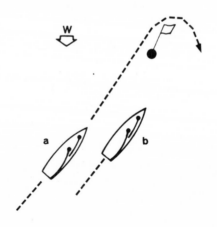

A.32. Since yacht A cannot tack to clear the obstruction, in this case shoreline, without affecting yacht B, yacht A is allowed to hail yacht B and ask for room to tack. See Rule 43.1 and 43.2.

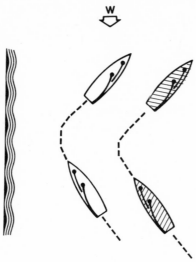

A.33. Yacht A is under no obligation to give yacht B room, and, accordingly, she should immediately inform yacht B to this effect. Yacht B must either ease her sheets and let yacht A pass, or do a 360-degree turn and cross yacht A's stern on the opposite tack. See Rule 43.3.

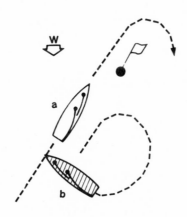

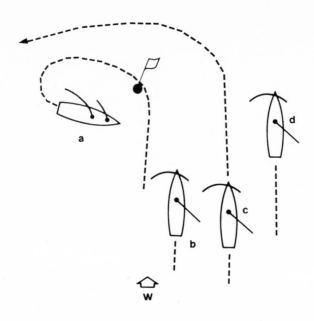

Q.34. Yacht A, in rounding the mark, touched it, and has begun her rerounding maneuver. She approaches yachts B, C, and D, all of which are on port tack, while A is on starboard tack. Who has right of way?

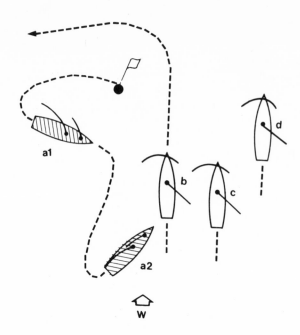

A.34. Yacht A, despite the fact she is on starboard tack, has no rights over any other yacht racing. She must alter her course to go astern of all other yachts so as not to interfere with them until she has completed her rounding maneuver correctly. See Rule 45.1.

3

Start

In an unenviable position, on the wrong side of the line with no place to go, is 12052, in this crowded Lightning start sequence. At the flag end, Photo 1 (BELOW), 12042 has trimmed sheets to force 11739 up into the wind (Rule 40). In Photo 2 (OPPOSITE, TOP) she has borne off and headed for the flag before she had to. Were she early, 12042 could have eased sheets without changing course. Just after the gun, Photo 3 (OPPOSITE, MIDDLE), 12042 still has enough way on to have saved her position and cleared the starting mark, and, once she trims her jib and gets going, she may still have a "safe leeward" on the fleet. Thirty seconds later (Photo 4, BOTTOM OPPOSITE), with the leaders off and running in what appears to be a freshening breeze, 12047 has unburied herself, tacked to port, and is heading for the windward side of the course looking for clear air and a chance to get back in the race. (Photos: ILCA)

Q.1. What are the three basic weapons a yacht in the lead can use in defending its position?

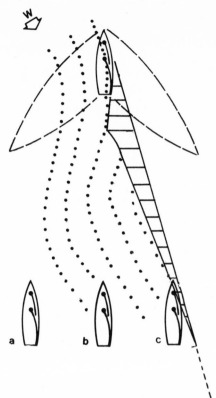

A.1. A leading yacht, hard on the wind, can employ its wind blanket, its backwind, and its wake as offensive weapons against following boats.

The wind blanket is a cone of disturbed wind extending astern and to leeward of a yacht's sails.

The effectiveness of this wind blanket depends on the amount of sail area and the height of the mast, together with the velocity of wind and the angle of sail trim. It can be from two to more than four boat lengths long.

Backwind, or deflected wind off the leading yacht's sails, is more general in nature and covers a greater area. A yacht not in the blanketing cone may nevertheless be influenced by backwind; a yacht dead astern, or even astern and slightly to weather, can also be affected by this disturbed air. Backwind is shown in the diagram as a series of dotted lines.

The leading yacht's bow waves and quarter waves have an effect on a yacht attempting to pass either to windward or to leeward. In the illustration shown above, yacht A is least af-

139

fected by the leading yacht, and if she's careful not to fall off too far to leeward she may be able to pass the lead yacht by superior sail trim and helmsmanship. Yachts B and C are in a very difficult position, however, and in most cases the leading yacht will gain enough on these two yachts so that they will have no chance to attack.

Experts like Dr. Curry and, more recently, Marchaj, have written about tests done to measure wind currents deflected by a boat's sails, the so-called wind blanket. They have concluded that the wind blanket area should no longer be considered an area of wind *vacuum,* but more properly an area of both turbulent wind currents, or eddies, and *deflected* wind currents.

Within the wind blanket formed by the sails of a yacht sailing close-hauled there are deflected wind currents which cause a following yacht sailing in this wind blanket area to sail in a so-called "header," or on a course that diverges slightly to leeward of the leading yacht.

On a dead-downwind run, the wind blanket extending from two to four boat-lengths ahead contains a much higher percentage of turbulent air and eddies, and a smaller percentage of the deflected wind currents found in the blanket of a yacht sailing close-hauled.

The total wind blanket/backwind area surrounding a yacht's sails is irregular in shape, and varies according to the wind velocity, the number and size of sails, the trim of the sails, the speed of the yacht, and even the amount of pitch and roll.

A yacht's sails not only affect wind currents directly astern, to leeward and behind, and slightly off the weather quarter; they actually *bend* the wind in front of and off the leeward bow of a yacht as well. These currents are deflected in such a way as to "lift" a yacht sailing in a position slightly ahead and to leeward (the so-called "safe leeward" position).

One thing is certain: a yacht's sails distort and/or "bend" wind currents as those currents are "used" by the sails to propel a yacht forward through the water. Any competitive yacht

140

directly behind, to leeward and astern, or even astern and to windward, will be adversely affected by sailing in these currents. On the other hand, a yacht in the "safe leeward" position will benefit from these "bent" wind currents by being "lifted" to a slightly higher angle of sail.

Q.2. What is the "safe leeward" position?

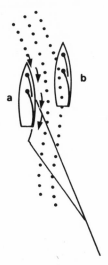

A.2. In this illustration, yacht A is still being backwinded by yacht B despite the fact that she is no longer clear astern of yacht B. Yacht B is therefore in a "safe leeward" position. Yacht A's sails are being adversely affected by deflected wind from yacht B's sails. If yacht A were to gain on yacht B so that her bow was approximately abeam of yacht B's bow, she might no longer be affected by backwind and could gain the advantage in this duel.

Q.3. What is the best starting position if the first leg is a beat to windward?

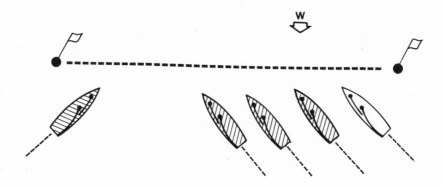

A.3. In the illustration above, the white yacht is starting in the best possible position. She is on starboard tack and she is at the windward end, from which position she will then be able easily to clear her wind by a short tack onto port (and then back onto starboard if she so desires).

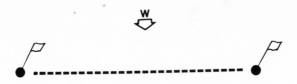

Q.4. Where would you start if the favored end of the line, as shown in answer 3, was too crowded?

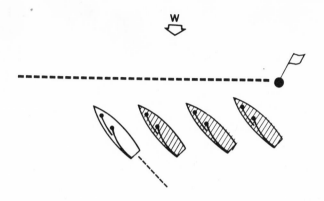

A.4. About 25 per cent of the way down the line from the starboard end. In starting at this position, it is most important that you time your start perfectly, and that you hit the line with full way on at the exact second the starting signal is given. Otherwise, yachts to windward of you may be able to gain clear air and overtake you. More important, yachts to leeward may be able to luff you and/or backwind you, thereby slowing your progress. If and when this occurs, you cannot tack and clear your air, since you will have other yachts to windward of you. The exact spot at which to cross the line is the spot where there is a "hole" in the pack of competing yachts and where there appears to be clear air.

Note: The first two minutes after the starting signal is given are among the most critical two minutes in any yacht race. Those first minutes will determine which yachts will sail in clear air and which yachts will sail in disturbed air. That critical period will also determine which yachts will sail to the side of the course they have selected as preferable, and which yachts will be forced, by clearing their air, to sail in a different area of the race course than they would ordinarily select.

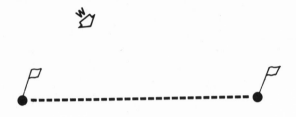

Q.5. In the above diagram, which is the preferred starting position?

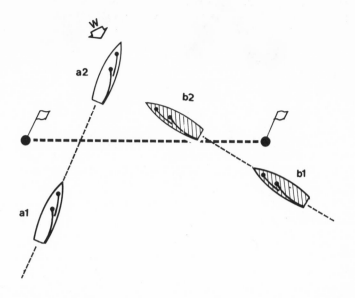

A.5. When the starting line is not square to the wind, i.e., when the wind direction is not 90 degrees to the line, one end of the line becomes favored. In this illustration, the wind favors the port tack (or left) end of the line, and a start at this end would be more advantageous. As you can see, a yacht on port tack, starting at position A1, will be ahead of a starboard tack yacht, starting at position B1, by the time the two yachts get to positions A2 and B2.

The danger in this maneuver is the fact that a port tack yacht does not have right-of-way over a starboard tack yacht. Therefore, any yacht on starboard tack at the port end of the line would be able to force the yacht in position A1 to either tack or to go astern of the starboard tack yacht (or yachts).

In a large fleet, a port tack start as illustrated would be very risky and probably nearly impossible. In multi-fleet regattas, it is often possible to watch other yachts from other classes during their starting procedure, to try to determine which end of the starting line appears to be favored. Many times, largely through habit, a large portion of the fleet will gather at the starboard end of the line when, in fact, a port end start is favored. When this happens, and you are able to get to the port end before the gun, you can pull off the yachts-

149

man's dream: an uncontested start at the favored end of the line, with full way on and clear air.

On the other hand, there may be times when, as you try to sneak off unobtrusively on port tack at the port end of the line, you will be caught "red-handed" by a number of yachts reaching down the starting line on starboard tack, with right-of-way over you and all other port tack yachts. If this happens, you'll probably have to ease sheets and duck under a number of yachts, look for a hole, tack quickly, and take your licking. Or, you may have to sail under most of (or the entire) fleet on port tack before you can tack in clear air.

OPPOSITE, TOP: *Shields Class yachts just prior to the starting signal. Some have been reaching down the starting line on starboard tack, hardening up as they see an opening. Yacht in foreground (65, although her number is not visible) appears to have clear air and has begun her final run to the line (Photo 1).* (Photo: Schwarm and Sheldon Inc.)

Shortly after the start (Photo 2, BOTTOM OPPOSITE), Shields 65 is sailing in clear air with good leeward position on the rest of the fleet, while 39 is sailing in disturbed air, is blanketed, and will probably be forced to tack to get free. If the breeze lifts, 65 will not be in a very good position, whereas a header will improve her position on the fleet, perhaps enabling her to tack and cross ahead of many competitors. (Photo: Stanley Rosenfeld)

Melee at the flag end of a Finn start! Apparently, too many yachts attempted to start on starboard tack at the flag. Those early were left with no place to go. Note the advantage of sailing in undisturbed air (especially in light wind conditions) as demonstrated by the port-tack yachts in the background.

OPPOSITE: *A sticky wicket among Class C cruising yachts at the start of the 1967 Nassau Cup Race. "Vela," 1430 on starboard tack, is pinching and trying to lay the leeward end of the starting line (out of sight at left). Her tactics have forced "Lively Lady" (976) and "Alegria" (1838) to head up in turn in order to keep clear. All three yachts narrowly escaped port tacking the entire starting fleet. (Photo: Frederic Maura, Bahamas Ministry of Tourism)*

153

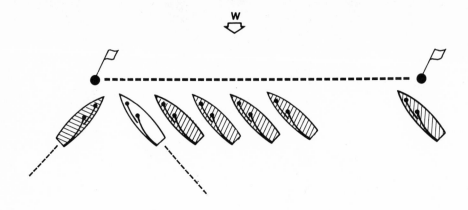

Q.6. What are the advantages and disadvantages of the start illustrated?

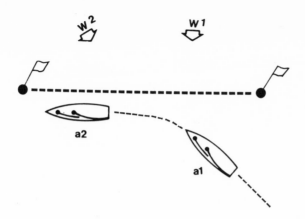

A.6. *Advantages:* (1) By starting on starboard tack at the leeward end of the line, you hinder all port tack starters attempting to start at this location. (2) If you have properly timed your start, and crossed the line at the leeward end exactly when the gun goes off, with full way on, you will have an advantageous, safe leeward position on all the boats at your end of the line. And (3) with good helmsmanship and sail trim you should be able to open up and pull ahead of these boats as you sail out to windward.

Disadvantages: (1) If you are late, another yacht can dip under you and force you up into the wind and possibly over the line before the starting signal. (2) If you are early, and try to slow down by luffing your sails, you can also be forced up and over the line early by leeward yachts. (3) If you do not have full way on, at the time you cross the line at the gun, yachts to windward, which *do* have full way on, will be able to pass you and blanket you; if this happens you will probably not be able to tack to clear your wind. (4) If you are forced over early by a leeward yacht there is no easy way for you to dip the line in order to restart. And (5) (Illustrated) In a backing-wind situation (wind changing in a counterclockwise direction, as in W-2) you may find as you get to the leeward end of the line (position A2) that you can no longer cross the line on starboard tack.

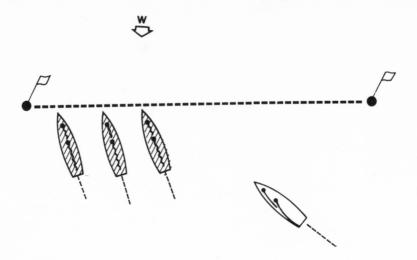

Q.7. What should you do if you are preparing to start on starboard tack at the leeward (or left) end of the line and you notice that other yachts, preparing for the same start, have arrived early and are ahead of you?

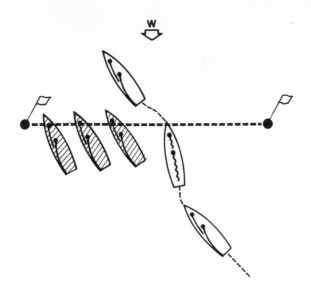

A.7. If the other yachts appear to be early reaching the leeward end of the line, you have an opportunity to change your course to windward, perhaps even luffing slightly if necessary, and cross the line well to windward of the yachts bunched at the leeward end. If you time this maneuver properly, you may still be able to cross the line with full way on, perhaps even overtaking and passing the other yachts since they were moving more slowly at the starting signal.

Q.8. What is the best start on a close reach?

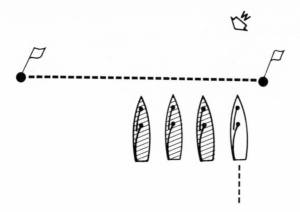

A.8. The best starting position in a close reach situation is at the windward end of the line, exactly at the starting signal and with full way on. From this position, especially if you are moving faster than competitors to leeward, you should be able to blanket them one by one as you gain steadily.

If you are late reaching the starting line, however, and your competitors to leeward have full way on, they will either start in or gradually work into a safe leeward position, from which they will backwind you and eventually pull out ahead.

If you are early approaching the line, and you are forced to slow down so as not to cross the line prematurely, and your competitors do not suffer from the same problem, they will break through your lee (particularly if yours is a heavier, keel-boat class where the yachts carry a lot of momentum) and gradually work out to windward, while backwinding you.

As the previous paragraph implies, if you cannot secure the windward boat position in this situation, full way on at the line at the gun in a leeward position is the next best start.

Q.9. Where should you start when the first leg is a beam reach?

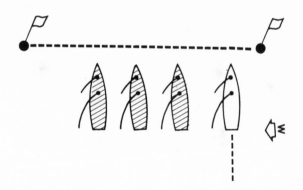

A.9. Since a beam reach is one of a sailboat's fastest points of sailing, you should plan to start at the windward end, as near the flag as possible, with full way on, crossing exactly at the starting signal. Your competitors will have difficulty establishing a safe leeward position when you are sailing on a beam reach, since their sails (and yours) will be eased.

Caution: In answers 8 and 9 note that before the start the white boat could easily be luffed to a course hard on the wind or even head to wind, by a leeward boat (Rule 40). She could even be forced to the wrong side of the starting mark (Rule 42.3). In answers 10 and 11, the same rules apply but the tactics may not be practical.

Finns just after the starting signal during the 1972 Olympics. US 337 is off and running, to windward of the fleet and in clear air. 888 has tacked to windward to clear her air, but will no doubt shortly return to starboard tack to cover the fleet. (Photo: Charles K. Hardy)

OPPOSITE: *International Tempest Class yachts 169 and 162 are both attempting the "perfect start" at the flag end of the line (Photo 1,* TOP). (Photo: Bob Lindgren)

In the second photo, taken approximately 20 seconds later (BOTTOM), *Tempest 162 has been able to work herself to windward and out of 169's backwind. Note flag end of line at far right of photo.* (Photo: Bob Lindgren)

162

163

Q.10. Where should you start on a broad reach?

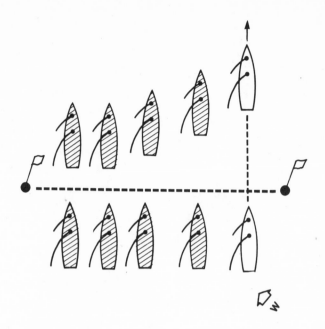

A.10. At the windward end of the starting line. But beware: downwind starts of this type can often lead to luffing matches (remember Rules 38.1 and 38.2).

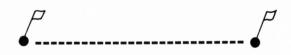

Q.11. Where should you start if it is a dead-downwind start?

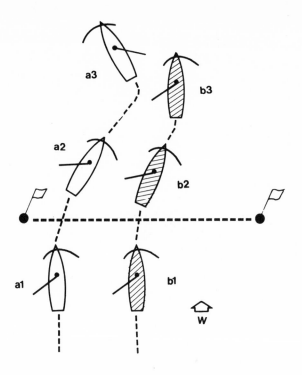

A.11. Preferably at the leeward end of the line. A yacht will very often move faster through the water if she is sailed 10 to 20 degrees off a dead downwind course. In the illustration above, assuming the next mark is dead downwind, a yacht starting as shown (A1) will be able to assume a faster sailing angle because of her leeward position, and thereby gain on her competitors. To reach the mark, she will eventually have to jibe several times from one very broad reach to another (called "tacking downwind"); but even though she will be sailing a greater distance than her competitors, her faster angle of sail may bring her to the next mark first.

Q.12. What is the ideal start regardless of angle of starting line to first mark, angle of starting line to the wind, number and position of competitors, etc.?

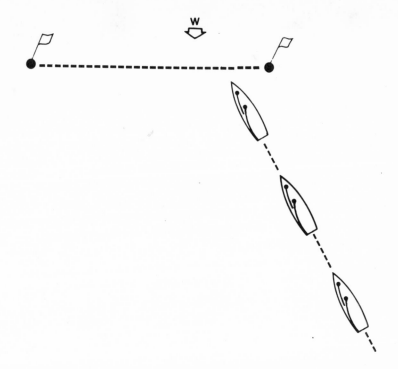

A.12. Crossing the line at the exact instant the starting signal is given with full boat speed and clear air. This kind of start will pay off for you handsomely in the first two minutes of the race. It is also, like the ninth inning grand-slam home run in baseball, every skipper's goal.

Q.13. What is the so-called "Vanderbilt" start?

Q.14. If too many boats are starting at the same place on the line, how can you use the "Vanderbilt" start system?

A.13. The "Vanderbilt" start is a timed run to the starting line from a predetermined distance behind the line. In a typical Vanderbilt start, you might begin by selecting the point on the line at which you wish to cross with four minutes, fifteen seconds to go. Sail away from this point for two minutes at an angle exactly opposite to the angle you will use to approach the line for your final run. At two minutes, either tack or jibe, then sail back on a reciprical course to your predetermined point on the line. If your tack or jibe has taken exactly fifteen seconds and the breeze holds steady, you will theoretically hit the line exactly as the starting signal is given, at the point you have previously selected and with full boat speed.

Some well-known and very successful skippers have refined the Vanderbilt start by employing a series of consecutive round-trip runs back and forth to the starting line prior to the starting signal. They normally use two-minute runs for larger yachts and one-minute runs for small boats. For instance, at six minutes to go, they may be at their pre-selected point on the line; at five minutes they have sailed away from the line and have tacked; at four minutes they are back at their pre-selected point on the line, etc., until they finally cross the line with zero time remaining. Throughout this six-minute series of runs (actually, three round trips) they are able to adjust their time, either for variances in wind speed, wind direction, wave action, or other yachts.

A.14. Change your selected point on the line to a spot perhaps 25 per cent of the way down the line from the crowded end, or perhaps at the opposite end of the line, and sail your dry runs from this position.

Q.15. After you have started your timed runs, you notice many boats sitting on the starting line with sails luffing. There seem to be too many boats for you to continue the normal Vanderbilt system. What should you do?

A.15. You may have to alter your timing so that you arrive back at the line a bit early, work your way into the pack, then sit and let your own sails luff. Beware of the luffing rule before the start (Rule 40), however, and do not let anyone get close to you to leeward. During the last thirty seconds before the starting signal, try to force yachts to windward of you further up, in order to create enough room so you can bear off and have clear air at the gun.

4

Windward Leg

Soling N 76 is locked between US 600 and D 46 during the 1972 Olympics. D 46 has a safe leeward, yet N 76 and US 600 do not seem to be seriously effected by D 46's backwind.

Lowell North of San Diego Yacht Club, a 1968 Olympic gold medalist, in Star 56, is working out into a "safe leeward" position. (Photo: Monk Farnham)

Heavy work to windward during the 1972 Dragon Olympic Trials. Taking a big dose of backwind is US 238.

Q.1. Is yacht A blanketing yacht B?

A.1. Yacht B is not blanketed, as the blanketing cone does not follow the direction of the true wind, but follows the direction of the apparent wind. In other words, the blanketing cone does not flow directly downwind from the leading yacht, but is affected by the leading yacht's forward speed, and therefore "bends" aft at an angle.

177

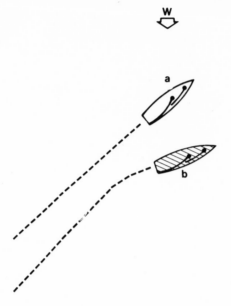

Q.2. Yacht B, sailing in yacht A's wind blanket, has begun to bear off to get clear air. What should yacht A do?

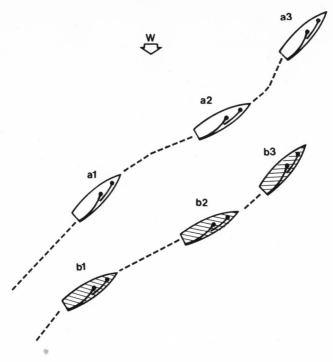

A.2. In a two-boat race, yacht A should also bear off temporarily in order to keep yacht B in her wind blanket. As yacht B falls further to leeward of yacht A, the blanketing cone will become less effective; at some point, yacht A should resume her close-hauled course to windward since she realizes her wind shadow is having little effect on yacht B. A basic tactical rule should be observed in such a case by yacht A: keep between your nearest competitor and the next mark. If yacht B tacks to get out of yacht A's wind blanket, yacht A should immediately tack in order to retain control.

In a large fleet, however, yacht A may have to continue on her optimum sailing angle regardless of what defensive actions any one individual competitor takes against her. In such situations, yacht A may not be able to devote her full attention to yachts following, and may be forced to tack to clear her own wind, even though it means allowing some competitors to go free . . . competitors she ordinarily would have covered.

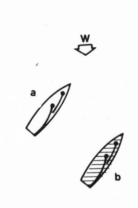

Q.3. What course should yacht A steer in this situation to be most effective against yacht B?

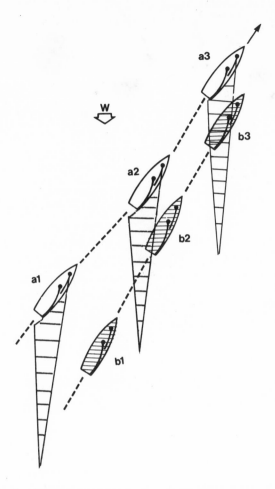

A.3. Yacht A should bear off to sail a freer course, thereby gaining speed and sailing up to windward and ahead of yacht B. As yacht A does this, yacht B will fall within A's wind blanket. Yacht A must be careful not to cause B to alter course, however, since she is windward yacht (Rule 37.1). As long as A's bow is even with, or slightly ahead of B when this maneuver begins, yacht A will probably be successful. Otherwise, B might be able to secure a safe leeward position on A, particularly if the two boats are close together.

Q.4. How should yacht B steer in the above situation?

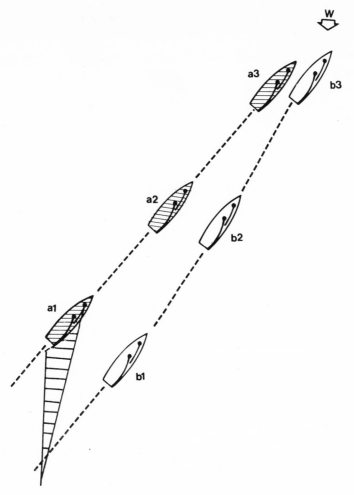

A.4. Yacht B should attempt to secure a safe leeward position. As she points up to converge with yacht A, however, she will slow down, and as she bears off away from yacht A, she will gain speed. She must watch yacht A's speed carefully so that she does not fall into yacht A's wind shadow while she works close up under A's bow. This will take skillful helmsmanship and sail trimming on yacht B's part. If yacht B determines she will *not* be able to secure a safe leeward position, and that yacht A will shortly blanket her, yacht B has no other recourse but to bear off and gain speed equal to yacht A's speed and sail along to leeward and slightly ahead of yacht A, and in clear air.

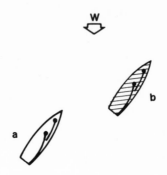

Q.5. How should yacht A attack yacht B?

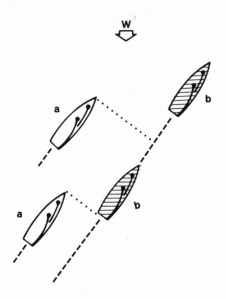

A.5. There is no effective way for yacht A to attack yacht B, but yacht A, at the first opportunity, should begin pointing higher than yacht B, therefore working into undisturbed air further to windward. Although this may cost her some distance along the course, it will prevent yacht B's being able to establish a safe leeward at some later date.

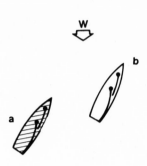

Q.6. How can yacht B attack yacht A?

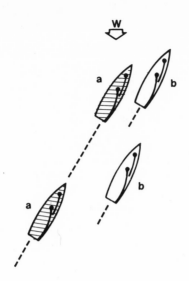

A.6. Yacht B should endeavor immediately to point as high as possible until she has secured a safe leeward on yacht A. From this position, she will have control over yacht A, and in the long run she will be able to work out into a considerable lead over A.

Q.7. Is it easier to break through the wind blanket of a yacht that is covering you when you are *close* to her or when you are further to leeward?

A.7. As the illustration shows, the further to leeward yacht B is sailing, the less the effect of the wind blanket. However, sailing too long a course around an opponent in order to avoid disturbed air is also a tactical error. The two conditions must be weighed against each other.

Q.8. Yacht B is being blanketed by yacht A. Each time yacht B tacks, yacht A tacks to cover. How can yacht B get away?

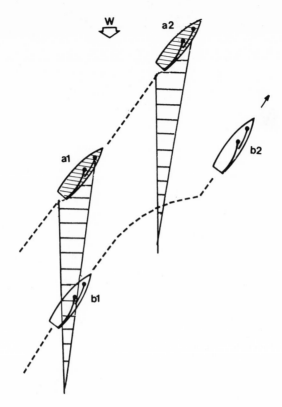

A.8. (a) The yacht being covered, yacht B in this case, should bear off enough to increase her speed, thereby trying to break through the wind blanket of yacht A. As she bears off she will fall to leeward and therefore pass through a smaller area of yacht A's wind blanket than she would if she continued her present course. If the maneuver is successful, yacht B will find herself further to leeward of yacht A, but in clear air and perhaps slightly ahead of her previous position, measured by sighting abeam. If yacht A also bears off, however, to continue to cover yacht B, yacht B's maneuver will not be successful.

(b) A second tactic is called the "False Tack," or "Fake Tack." Yacht B's skipper announces loudly to his crew that he is preparing to tack. He finally says "Hard alee" in a loud voice. At the same time, he puts the helm over slowly and heads straight into the wind. Yacht A will hear and observe this and will, hopefully, tack at about the same time. What

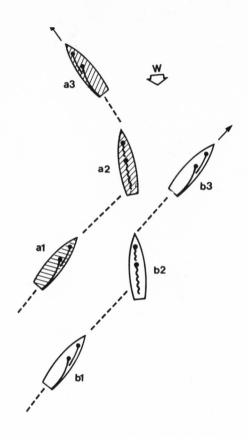

yacht A's helmsman does not know is that yacht B's skipper has previously warned his crew that he is *not* actually going to tack, but that this is instead a *fake* tack. If she sees that yacht A has completed her tack onto starboard, yacht B will *not* complete *her* tack, but will bear off again onto the original tack (port) and gain full way. If yacht B has been successful, yacht A will be on the opposite tack and yacht B will be sailing in clear air.

(c) A third method of attack is called the "Double Tack." The helmsman of yacht B should forwarn his crew that he is going to tack very quietly and very quickly. At the same time, he should also warn the crew that they must gain all possible boat speed immediately after the tack as there will probably be another tack very shortly. If yacht B is to maintain boat speed through two tacks this close together, her crew must be sure both tacks are conducted very efficiently. At the proper command, yacht B very quietly tacks, trying to time the tack so that the crew of yacht A is not looking. Yacht A will no doubt tack to cover quickly thereafter, however, and here comes yacht B's opportunity. As soon as A has completed her tack, B immediately tacks again. Since yacht A was not prepared for the first tack, it is a good assumption yacht A will be moving relatively slowly at the time yacht B tacks the second time. If yacht A *does* try to tack a second time to cover, she will be practically dead in the water and yacht B should be able to drive through her lee. Yacht A's skipper may well decide, however, that he does *not* have sufficient boat speed to tack again, in which case B has been successful in splitting tacks with A. In some classes of smaller dinghy-type boats, it may be very difficult to tack twice in a very short span of time. Here again, to be successful in this maneuver, as in many other cases in this book, the helmsman must know his boat and its capabilities to be successful.

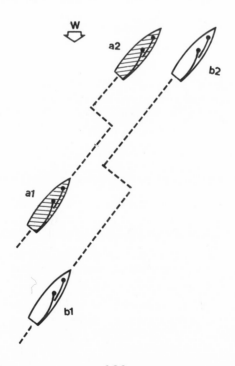

Despite the fact that International 14 is to leeward and slightly astern of 8, she is sailing in clear air at this point. (Photo: Fusanori Nakajima)

In this Bermuda Great Sound race, International One-Design 5 is tacking to get out of 8's wind blanket. (Photo: Gene Ray, Bermuda News Bureau)

During the America's Cup Trials, Intrepid (US 22) has a good wind-ward position on Valiant (US 24). (Photo: BOATFOTOS by Howey Caufman)

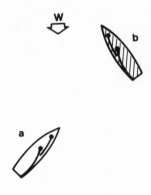

Q.9. What must yacht A anticipate that yacht B will do in this situation?

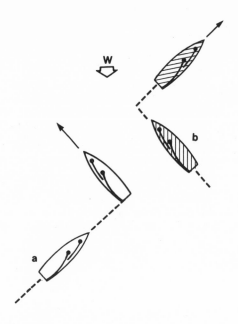

A.9. It is possible that yacht B will continue on starboard tack, in which case yacht A would remain in clear air without being forced to tack. Yacht A must anticipate, however, that unless yacht B elects to cover a larger portion of the fleet (perhaps because most of the fleet is remaining on starboard tack behind her), B will probably tack onto port to cover A. Yacht A's defense in this case is to tack immediately onto starboard so that she will be in clear air. It is unlikely that yacht B will tack back onto starboard immediately after her previous tack, for this would slow her down too severely. The result is that yacht A will be sailing on starboard in clear air and will have split tacks with yacht B.

Should yacht B tack twice in an attempt to cover yacht A, and end up back on starboard tack, she would find herself to windward of yacht A, but not far enough ahead to be able to cover A. This is illustrated below.

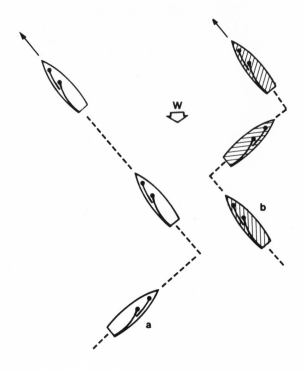

If yacht A, on port tack, determines that she wishes to remain on port tack . . . either to get to a pre-selected side of the course, or to cover following yachts, or to sail away from an unfavorable current, there is one tactic she may use in order to deceive the helmsman of yacht B. As yacht B is about to cross her bow, A can point up higher into the wind, sailing as high as she can possibly sail without having her sails actually luff. This may give the helmsman of yacht B the impression that A is sailing in a lift and that he should sail further beyond her before he tacks. If yacht B *does* continue further than he needs to, the minute B tacks A should immediately bear off and try to drive under B. Yacht A may thus sail into clear air, with increased boat speed, during the time yacht B is regaining her speed after the tack. If yacht B's skipper is not deceived and yacht A is not able to drive through yacht B's lee, as a last recourse, yacht A can tack onto starboard and hope that she can split tacks with yacht B.

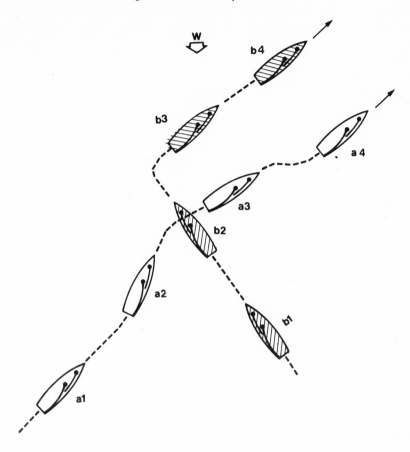

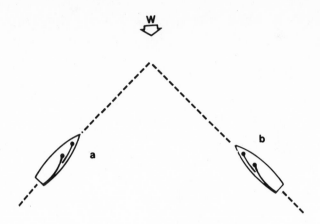

Q.10. What actions should yacht A and yacht B take, since both are on converging courses and are about equidistant from the potential point of collision?

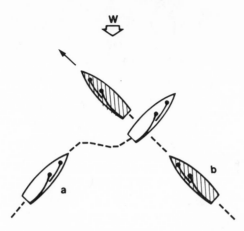

A.10. Yacht A, having no rights in this situation, must first decide which side of the course she wants to sail toward: does she prefer to stay on port tack, or would she rather sail on starboard tack? Favorable current, wind shifts observed affecting other yachts ahead, or competitors behind she wishes to cover could all be reasons for her selecting one side of the course instead of the other. If she elects to stay on port (illustration 1), yacht A should bear off under the stern of yacht B; when coming back to her close-hauled sailing course, she should try to point a little higher than normal for a short period of time, in effect utilizing the additional boat speed she gained by easing her sheets and driving under B's stern. When A is passing this close astern, B cannot tack to cover her or hinder her maneuver in any way.

If she elects to tack onto starboard (illustration 2), yacht A should do this before she gets too close to yacht B.

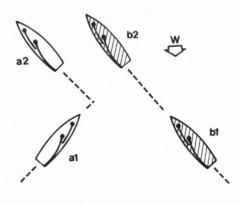

If yacht A waits too long before tacking, yacht B, having greater boat speed during the period of time A is tacking, will ride up on and blanket A after her tack (illustration 3).

Yacht B, however, is on starboard tack; she has right of way, and need not do anything but sail a straight course.

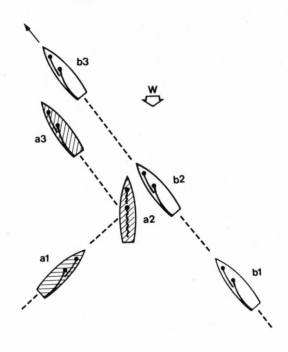

Sail trim and helmsmanship will determine which of these Finn skippers will work out ahead of his competitors. (Photo: George Smith)

International One-Design 2 is sailing high to keep clear of 8's backwind during a team race in Bermuda's Hamilton Harbour. (Photo: Gene Ray, Bermuda News Bureau)

A large fleet of Snipes works to windward during the 1972 Southern Snipe Championship at Chattanooga, Tennessee. (Photo: Cecil Pearce)

Her crew hiking out on the windward rail helps this 5.5-meter yacht work out on her opponents. (Photo: Frederic Maura, Bahamas News Bureau)

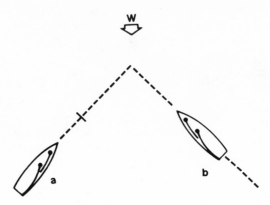

Q.11. What action should yacht A take in approaching yacht B in the above situation? (Yacht B is one-half boat length ahead.) How about yacht B, what action should she take?

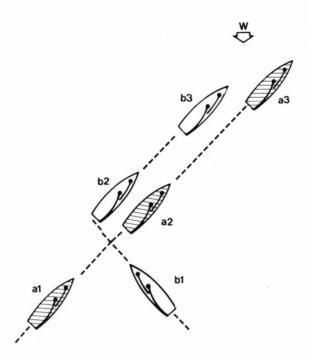

A.11. Yacht A, in this situation, can probably not successfully tack to leeward of yacht B and still avoid B's wind blanket. If yacht A *must* tack, she should do so quite early, since her chances of being blanketed are much greater than they were in answer 10 on the previous page. Yacht A's safest maneuver is to bear off under yacht B's stern and continue on port tack. Since yacht A will not have to bear off very much to clear yacht B's stern, she will not lose as much in this maneuver as she would in answer 10, particularly if B tacks to attempt to cover (see below).

Yacht B, on starboard tack, has rights over A. Yacht B merely has to continue on starboard tack and cross A's bow. If B wishes to cover A, her best maneuver is to tack to leeward of A, thereby gaining a safe leeward position. If B attempts to cover A by crossing A's bow and *then* tacking, she will find herself too far astern to affect yacht A with her wind blanket. Indeed, yacht A may well be able to backwind yacht B, if B has tacked too close (illustration 11).

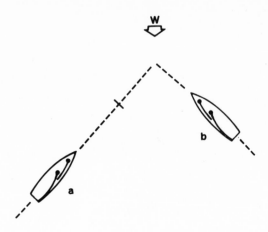

Q.12. What action should yacht A take in the above situation? What action should yacht B take? (B is one full boat length ahead.)

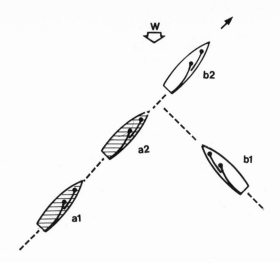

A.12. Yacht A, in this situation, will have to bear off very little, if at all, to clear yacht B's stern. Holding her course is A's best maneuver, as described in the previous answer.

Yacht B, on starboard tack, can either continue on starboard and cross A's bow, or she can tack slightly to leeward and ahead of yacht A (being careful to observe Rule 41.1), and force A into her wake (illustration 12). Yacht A, under these conditions, will be in a bad backwind situation.

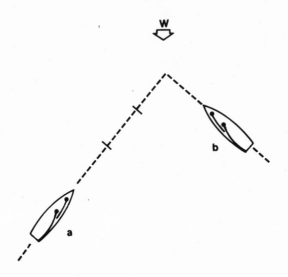

Q.13. What is yacht A's proper maneuver in this situation? Yacht B's? (Yacht B is two boat legnths ahead.)

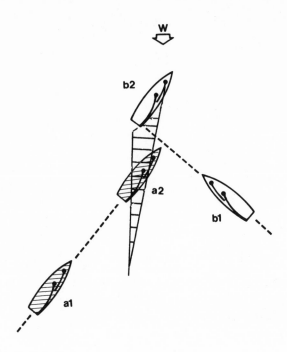

A.13. Yacht A could tack immediately and not suffer any blanketing effect from yacht B. Yacht A could also maintain her present course and clear B's stern with no necessity to bear off. If yacht A elects to continue on port tack, however, she must watch out that yacht B does not tack on her and blanket her as she attempts to cross B's stern.

Yacht B can continue on starboard tack, or she can tack ahead and slightly to windward of yacht A, thus placing A in her blanket zone. Yacht B, in this maneuver, although she is on starboard tack and thus has rights over yacht A, must be very careful not to tack too close to A (again note Rule 41.1).

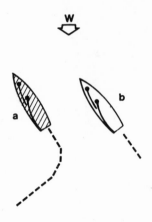

Q.14. Yacht A has just tacked to leeward and slightly ahead of yacht B. What is yacht B's best maneuver in this situation?

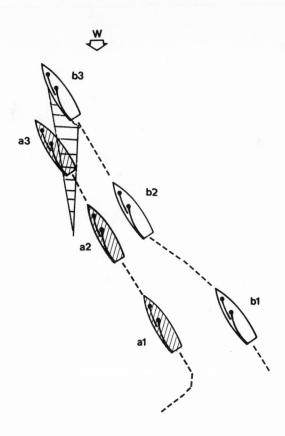

A.14. Since yacht B has room to bear off and gain speed, she should attempt to do so. Yacht B should begin this maneuver as soon as yacht A has completed her tack. If yacht B is unable to bear off and gain sufficient speed to pull slightly ahead of yacht A, B should immediately prepare to tack, for yacht A may begin to backwind B and will thus secure a safe leeward position. Caution: yacht B, in getting close to yacht A in this situation, is running a very dangerous risk of being luffed suddenly by A while yacht A has luffing rights (Rule 38.1 and 38.2).

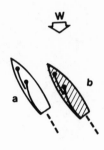

Q.15. What should yacht A do if yacht B tacks?

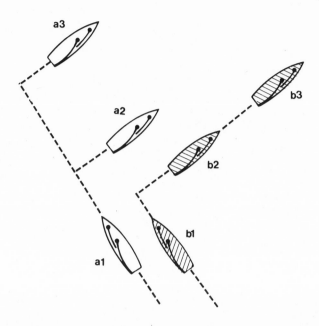

A.15. Yacht A must continue on her present course for at least two and preferably three boat lengths before she tacks. If yacht A were to tack too soon after B's tack, she would fall into yacht B's backwind and would have gone from a safe leeward position, before the tack, to a backwinded position, as in positions A2 and B2. Yacht A must continue on her present course for at least two boat lengths before she tacks, so that she will be sailing in clear air (A3, B3).

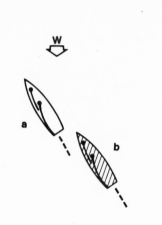

Q.16. What should yacht A do in this situation if yacht B tacks?

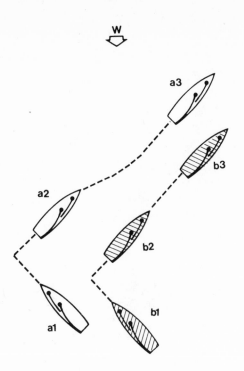

A.16. Once yacht B tacks, yacht A should tack immediately and bear off quickly so as to gain the greatest amount of speed in the shortest possible period of time. By doing this, yacht A may be able to override yacht B to windward and place B in her wind blanket. Remember that in this situation yacht B was probably not sailing as fast as yacht A before the tack, since yacht B was sailing in yacht A's backwind, which is the reason A may well be able to overhaul B to windward as described above. (Again, observe Rule 37.1.)

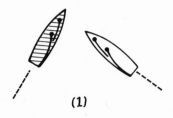

(1)

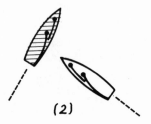

(2)

Q.17. How can the two yachts maneuver so as to avoid a collision in Situation One and in Situation Two?

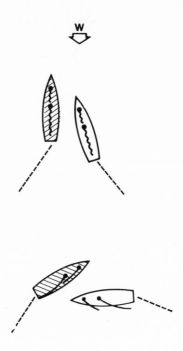

A.17. In Situation One the collision can be avoided if both yachts immediately go head-to-wind. As a general rule, if the point of collision between the two yachts would be forward of amidships on one of the yachts, both should luff head-to-wind.

In Situation Two both yachts should bear off as quickly as possible to avoid a collision.

In both of these situations, however, the port tack yacht has fouled the starboard tack yacht, whether there is a collision or not.

Q.18. How can yacht A improve her position when covered closely by yacht B as in the above situation?

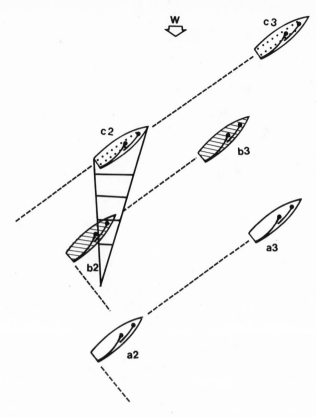

A.18. Yacht A should tack, which might induce her nearest competitor, yacht B, to tack in yacht C's wind blanket while trying to cover A.

If yacht B tacks to cover (illustrated above), B will sail in yacht C's wind blanket, while yacht A sails in clear air and should thus gain.

On the other hand, if yacht B realizes what A is trying to do and does *not* tack, A will have split tacks with B and will be sailing in clear air.

a

Q.19. If the mark is dead to windward of yacht A, how should A proceed in the above situation?

A.19. Since both her opponents are equidistant behind her, and sailing on opposite tacks, yacht A has a difficult choice to make. If one side of the course seems favored over the other (perhaps a stronger wind or favorable tide, etc.), this could be a factor in her decision. If one of her two competitors is closer in the series standings than the other, yacht A may decide to cover her closest competitor. Perhaps one of the following yachts is sailed by a better skipper than the other, in which case yacht A might then decide to cover the better skipper and take his chances with the other yacht.

If there is still no clear choice, yacht A should remain pretty much in the center of the course without sailing out as far on either tack as her competitors. At the same time she should watch for any clue that could lead her to feel she should cover one competitor more closely. Yacht A should keep in mind that each time she tacks she loses up to a boat length of distance, and thus should not tack any more often than necessary.

a

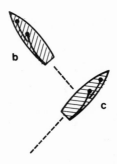

b

c

Q.20. In the above diagram, how should yacht A proceed, assuming the next mark is directly to windward?

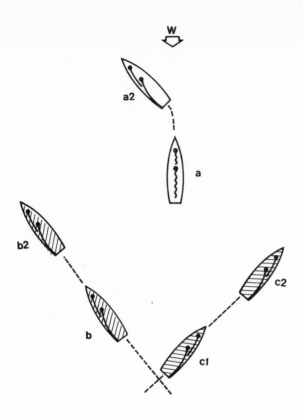

A.20. Yacht A should cover her nearest opponent. In this case she should cover the starboard tack yacht, yacht B.

Ideally, yacht A wants both her competitors on the same tack; so, to encourage B to tack, A should harass B as much as possible with her wind blanket.

If and when yacht B *does* tack, yacht A should cover both B and yacht C loosely, thus encouraging both to stay on the same tack rather than forcing one of them to split and go off on the other tack again.

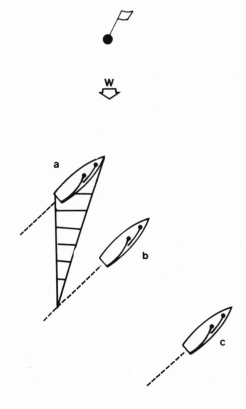

Q.21. In the above diagram should yacht A bear off and gain speed in order to more effectively cover yacht B? (Note the turning mark to windward of yacht A.)

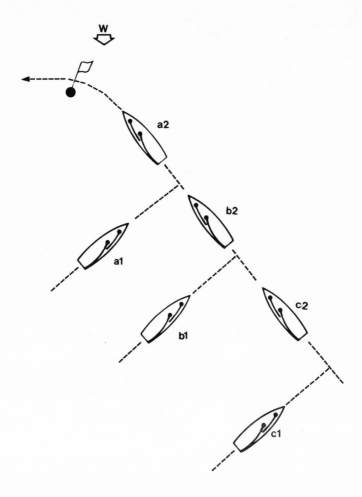

A.21. No. If yacht A bears off and eventually covers yacht B, she will merely force yacht B to tack onto starboard to clear her air. Yacht A can more effectively cover both competitors all the way to the turning mark if she loosely covers yacht B and encourages both B and C to sail to the lay line on port tack. Once all three yachts reach the lay line, they will tack onto starboard and head for the turning mark, whereupon yacht A will be in decisive control, via her backwind and her bow and stern waves.

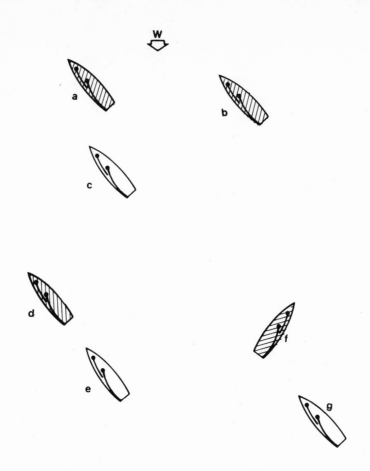

Q.22. In the above diagram, what course should yacht C take? What is the best maneuver for yacht E? And what is the proper maneuver for yacht G?

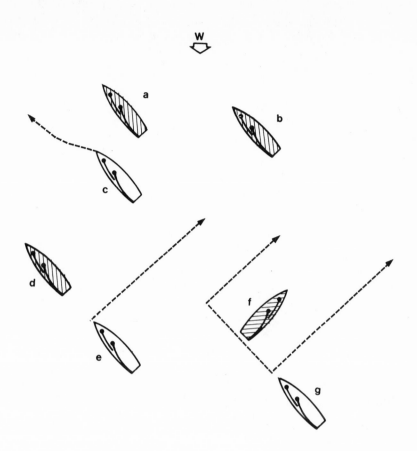

A.22. Yacht C should attempt to bear off, try to gain speed and sail into clear air to leeward and abeam of yacht A. If she is unable to do this, C should tack and cross on port tack astern of yacht B into clear air.

Yacht E has no choice except to tack, since she is in the backwind and disturbed water of yacht D.

Since yacht G is so far behind, and is sailing in disturbed air and water, she has everything to gain by splitting with the fleet and sailing off on port tack. If she tacks immediately, G might be blanketed by yacht F, so she might best decide to cross yacht F's wake by about two boat lengths before she tacks onto port.

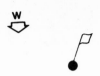

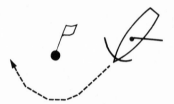

Q.23. After rounding the leeward mark, and assuming the distance to the next windward mark is one mile, which tack should this yacht first sail on, and what should be her proper course to the next mark?

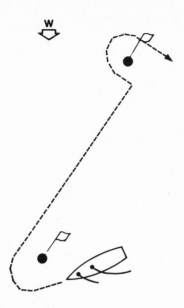

A.23. This yacht should tack onto port upon rounding the leeward mark. The final short starboard tack should be left for the windward end of the leg so as to eliminate any chance of overstanding due to an unforeseen windshift or current change.

Caution: Under certain extreme conditions of light breezes and disturbed sea, when it is difficult to maintain either momentum or steerage, it may be wise not to tack immediately after rounding the mark. A wise skipper will delay his tack until boat speed has been regained.

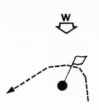

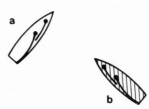

Q.24. What is the proper course for yacht A to sail from the above position?

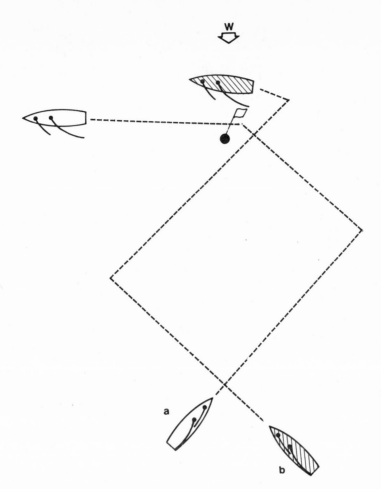

A.24. Yacht A should not tack in order to blanket or backwind her opponent when she is just a short distance from the windward mark, as shown in the illustration. Instead, she should proceed to the lay line before she tacks. Yacht B, on the other hand, will have to tack twice, which of course will cost her additional time.

Yacht A has another advantage in proceeding to the lay line before tacking: she will reach the windward mark on starboard tack, whereas yacht B will arrive on port tack with no rights. In the above situation, if yacht A did tack to cover yacht B, she would have to tack three times before rounding, meaning she would give up more of her lead than is necessary.

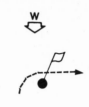

Q.25. In this illustration what course should yacht B choose, since the distance to the windward mark is not very great?

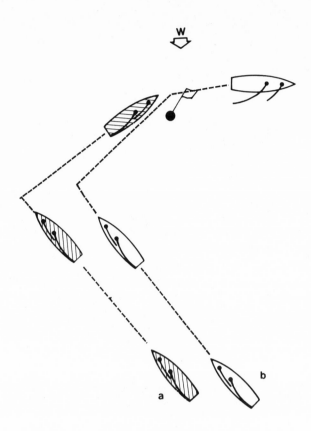

A.25. Yacht B should continue on her present course despite the fact she is being backwinded by yacht A. In the short distance remaining to the lay line, yacht A will be too close to yacht B to tack, even though she may be gaining, owing to the effect of her backwind on yacht B.

As shown in illustration 1, yacht B can arrive at the lay line and tack when she is sure she can comfortably lay the mark. Yacht A will not be able to tack until Yacht B has gone about. Yacht B thus arrives at the mark first, and should lead A on the next leg.

Illustration 2 shows what might happen if yacht B tacked to avoid yacht A's backwind. B was not moving as fast as A since she was sailing in A's backwind. She will also have to make one more tack than A before the two yachts converge near the mark. It is therefore reasonable to assume that, although B

will arrive at the mark on starboard tack, she will get there too late to use her starboard tack advantage, and yacht A will round ahead of her.

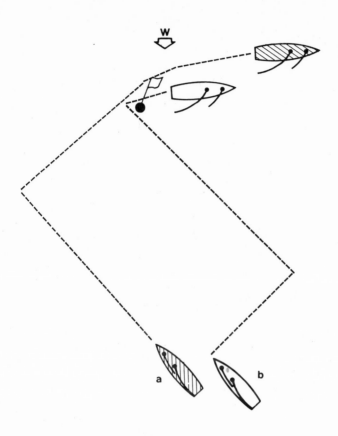

Q.26. In the above illustration, what is the proper maneuver for yacht B? (Both yachts are approximately one-half mile from the windward mark.)

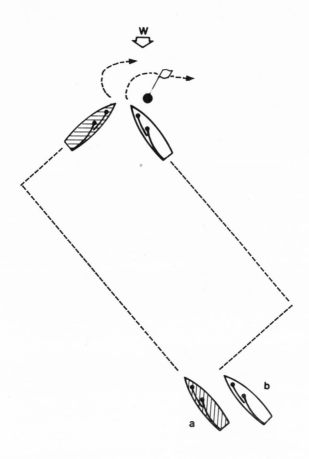

A.26. This question differs from the preceding question only in the greater distance of the yachts from the windward mark. Since yacht B is sailing in yacht A's backwind, and will lose ground steadily to A, the length of time she stays in this position becomes important in determining which boat will round the windward mark first.

Since greater distance is involved yacht B should tack onto port. Both yachts will sail the same distance to the mark, but yacht B will make two more tacks than yacht A. Since yacht B is arriving at the mark on starboard tack, this advantage may make up for her additional tack. In any case, she has no choice; to sail in yacht A's backwind for that great a distance

would ensure her arrival at the mark behind A. Illustration 1 shows what yacht B *should* do; illustration 2 shows what would happen to her if she continued in yacht A's backwind.

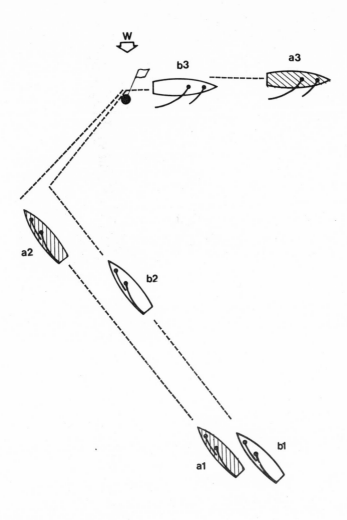

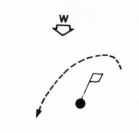

Q.27. How should yacht B maneuver so as to gain on yacht A?

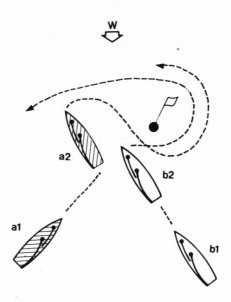

A.27. Yacht B, on starboard tack, is in a position to force yacht A to tack, thus driving A away from the mark. Yacht B can then tack, sail directly for the mark, and round well ahead of yacht A.

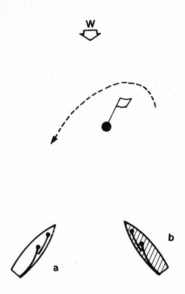

Q.28. What maneuver could yacht A perform to avoid being forced to tack away from the mark?

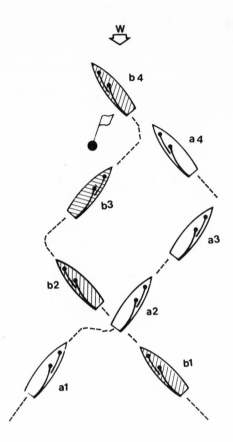

A.28. If yacht A sees she cannot cross yacht B's bow without fouling B, and if she sees that yacht B intends to hold her course and force A to tack, yacht A should seriously consider bearing off under yacht B's stern. She would thereby lose a little distance to windward, but could then tack on her new lay line and approach the mark on starboard tack. She would generally lose less in this maneuver than if she had been forced about by yacht B before rounding.

245

5
Reaching

Shields Class yachts close-reaching on Long Island Sound. National champions Richard and James Sykes (64) are endeavoring to stay between competitors Herman Whiton, Sr. (38) and Robert Garland (82), and the next mark. (Photo: Stanley Rosenfeld)

OPPOSITE: *Cruising yachts reaching during the 1965 Miami-Nassau race.* (Photo: Frederic Maura, Bahamas Ministry of Tourism)

247

Q.1. Where does the blanketing cone form when a yacht is reaching, as shown in the illustration?

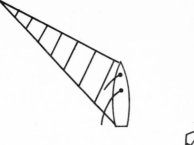

A.1. The blanketing cone is formed to leeward of the yacht in a direction opposite that of the *apparent* wind, not the true wind, as you might expect. Furthermore, the faster a yacht is moving, the further *forward* the apparent wind moves, and the further *aft* the blanketing cone will be bent.

Wind pennants on a yacht, especially at masthead, will show the apparent wind and will indicate the actual direction to leeward that the blanketing cone will form.

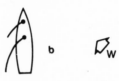

Q.2. How should yacht B attack yacht A so as to pass her?

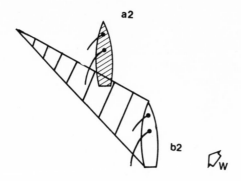

A.2. In order to make the best use of her blanketing cone, yacht B should pass yacht A to windward and as close as possible. Yacht B's wind blanket will thus be most effective in slowing yacht A's speed so that B will be able to pass her. By sailing slightly high of her present course she will gradually bring her wind blanket to bear on yacht A's sails. In passing close aboard, however, yacht B will be hindered by yacht A's quarter wave, and of course she will be sailing a longer course than yacht A. Yacht B must also remember that in passing yacht A to windward she may be luffed by A.

Q.3. How may yacht B defend herself from being overtaken by yacht A?

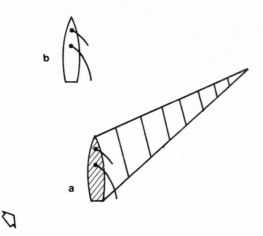

A.3. By sailing a slightly higher course to the position shown in illustration 1. In the illustration accompanying the question yacht A has not yet blanketed yacht B. Assuming that the rhumb line course to the next mark is straight to the top of the page, yacht B can sail a slightly higher course than yacht A and cross in front of A. Upon squaring away to her true course, B will be slightly to windward and ahead of A. In this position she can hinder A from trying to pass to leeward, because of B's quarter wave, backwind, and wind blanket. If yacht A attempts to pass to windward, yacht B can luff A, as shown in illustration 2, and still keep her wind clear.

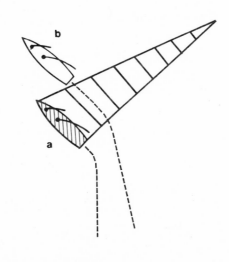

Q.4. How can yacht A gain on yacht B?

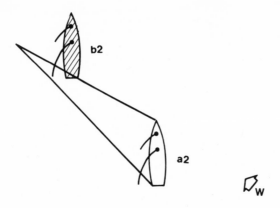

A.4. Yacht A is too far away from yacht B to effectively blanket her, being approximately three boat lengths directly astern. Yacht A must therefore place great emphasis on sail trim, weight distribution, and helmsmanship in order to gradually close the distance on B. In the illustration above, yacht A has gained enough on yacht B (she is now less than one boat length astern), and has moved up enough to windward, for her wind shadow to now be effective in slowing yacht B. However, yacht A must work up to windward very gradually, or she will sail too long a course, and perhaps lose some of the distance she may have gained through better helmsmanship.

The windward 5.5-meter yacht is "knocked down" by this gust while attempting to pass several competitors. US 42 is driving off and handling it nicely.

Tempests after rounding a jibe mark during the 1972 Olympic Trials. 214 elected to sail high of the next mark, worked out to windward of her competitors (and out of their disturbed air) and won this race. (Photo: Bob Lindgren)

A close reach during a 5.5-meter regatta in Hamilton Sound, Bermuda. US 68 has lost his spinnaker. Note the luffing match between US 72 and his competitor, which has caused US 72's spinnaker to collapse. (Photo: Frederic Maura, Bahamas News Bureau)

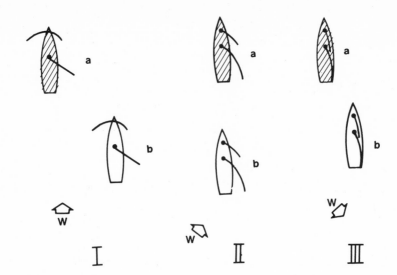

I   II   III

Q.5. How should yacht B attempt to break through yacht A's lee in each of the above illustrations? Which of the three maneuvers is the easiest to perform?

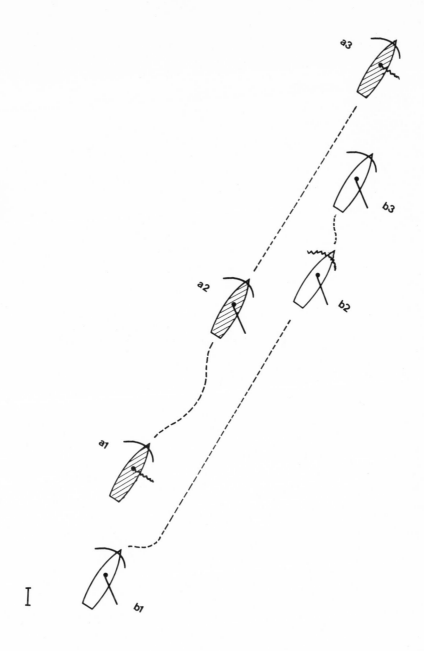

A.5. In illustration 1, yacht B1 is easily able to blanket yacht
A1, change her course to leeward, and pass A. As can be seen,

however, once passed, yacht A can in turn bear off, blanket yacht B and then pass her (positions A2, B2.) So you might say this is the easiest way to pass to leeward, but the "least permanent."

In illustration 2, it will be almost impossible for yacht B to pass yacht A to leeward. First of all, A's wind blanket is particularly wide at this angle of sailing, so that B will have to go quite far to leeward in order to break through. Sailing this far to leeward, however, B will sail a significantly longer course than A, as can be seen. So yacht B must not only sail faster than yacht A; she must also sail a longer course to ultimately sail through A's wind blanket: a most difficult maneuver.

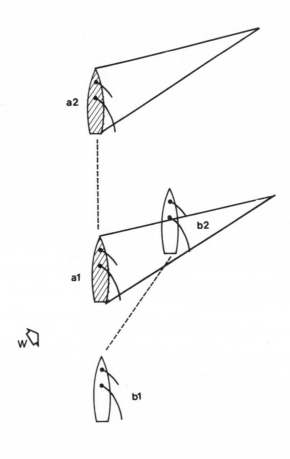

II

In illustration 3, yacht B is being partially blanketed by yacht A. Assuming this blanketing has just begun, and B's speed has not yet been seriously affected by A's blanket, B must bear off quickly in order to gain more speed and thus sail through A's blanket. This can probably be done if B acts quickly . . . before her speed is seriously affected by the blanketing cone. B will thus in effect trade distance to windward for increased speed, and may ultimately break out into clear air to leeward of yacht A.

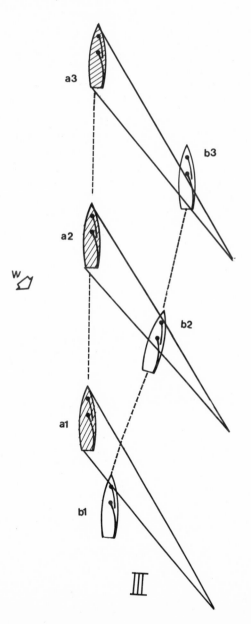

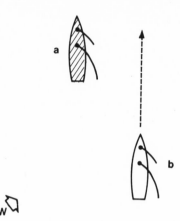

Q.6. If breaking through the lee of another yacht when she is on a broad reach is a very difficult maneuver, then under what special circumstances can the task be made easier for a trailing yacht?

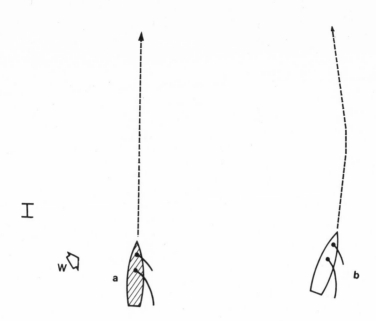

A.6.(a) A long course gives yacht B a better opportunity to break through to leeward. She needs only bear off very slightly from the rhumb line course to be able to sail far enough to leeward of yacht A so as to avoid her wind shadow completely, as in illustration 1.

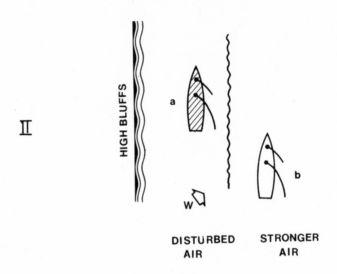

(b) If both yachts A and B are sailing close to the shore-line, particularly one with high bluffs or trees, yacht B might well be able to sail further away from the shore and not have her wind obstructed by the trees or bluffs. Yacht B would therefore be sailing in stronger wind than yacht A and should be able to break through her lee more easily, as in illustration 2.

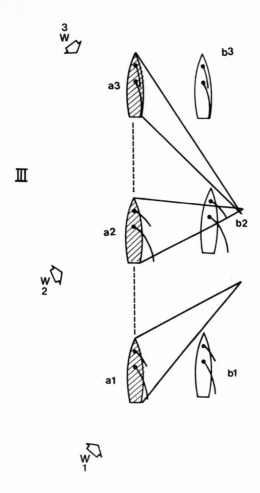

(c) Veering winds can become a big advantage under certain conditions. As you can see from illustration 3 if yacht B is sailing the same course as yacht A, and to leeward of A, and the wind shifts to a more forward position, yacht B may find herself sailing in clear wind ahead of yacht A's blanket instead of astern of yacht A's blanket.

All three of these illustrations are highly theoretical, yet in varying degrees they can and do influence the outcome of yacht races.

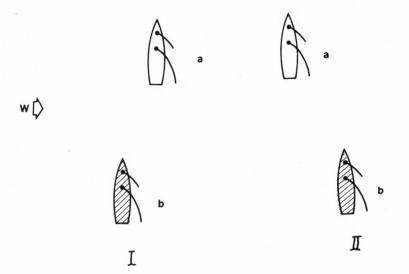

Q.7. In which illustration is yacht A in the stronger defensive position?

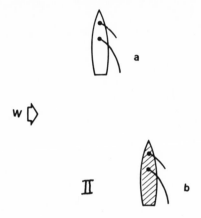

A.7. Both positions are good. Being to windward, however, as in illustration 2, yacht A has several advantages: (1) Yacht B cannot break through A's lee very easily, inasmuch as A's stern waves, backwind, and wind blanket will all decrease yacht B's speed. (2) Yacht B cannot easily sail higher than yacht A in order to try to pass to windward, since A is *already* to windward and does not need to sail as high a course to *stay* to windward. (3) If the wind shifts forward, A will have B even more effectively backwinded. (4) If the wind shifts aft, B will still have to sail through A's wind blanket in order to pass.

a

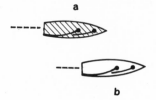

b

Q.8. Describe the techniques of luffing an opponent who is attempting to pass you to windward from clear astern.

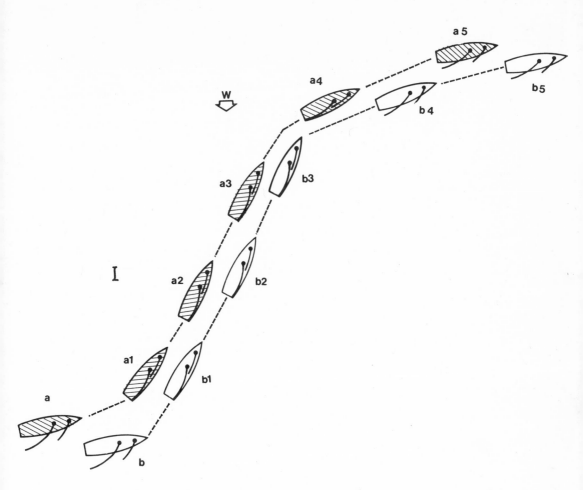

A.8. In illustration 1, you see a normal luffing match. Yacht B is being overtaken to windward by yacht A, at which point B luffs A by sailing close enough to the wind for her back-wind to take effect. B will thus slow yacht A sufficiently to enable B to move out ahead. At this point, yacht B should bear off and resume her course to the next mark.

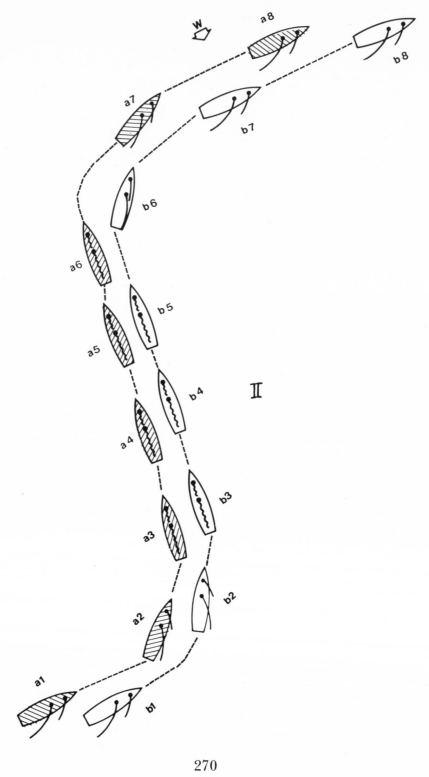

II

In illustration 2, we see an extreme luffing match where yacht B has luffed yacht A head-to-wind. Both yachts will gradually lose momentum. When yacht B feels her speed has slowed sufficiently that she may be starting to lose steerage way, she should suddenly bear off toward the next mark and trim sail so as to gain speed as quickly as possible. Yacht A must leave sufficient room between hulls so that when yacht B bears off there will be no contact. Yacht A's speed will *also* be slowed by this maneuver; nevertheless she must not bear off until yacht B does so. At this point, yacht A's speed may be practically zero, and her turn back to her previous course will be much slower. Yacht B should therefore be able to open up a considerable lead.

6

Running

OPPOSITE: *Finn BL 3 should round this leeward mark in first place, while US 868 may have to give room at the mark to the Finn behind the flag.*

272

Solings rounding a leeward mark in San Francisco Bay. 296 is jibing well, with spinnaker full and main just coming around.

W

Q.1. Where does the blanketing cone lie when a yacht is running before the wind? How far does it reach?

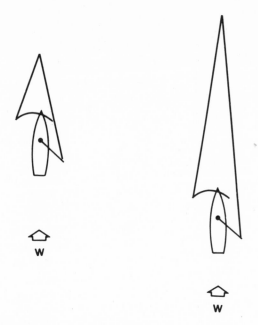

A.1. The blanketing cone extends directly downwind of a yacht, if the yacht is sailing directly before the wind. In light breezes, it extends to a distance of one or two boat lengths; in heavier breezes it may extend as far as four boat lengths.

Q.2. How should the yacht astern attempt to pass her opponent?

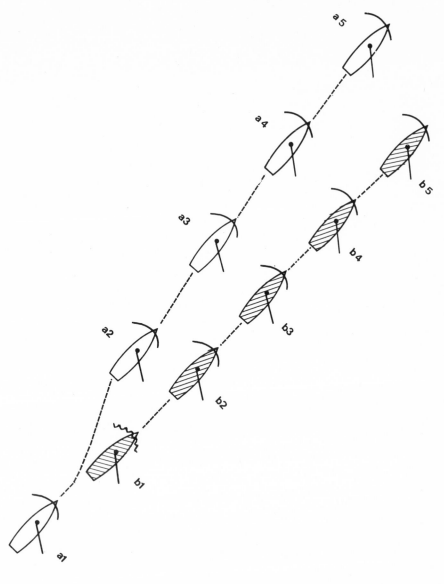

A.2. Yacht A should blanket yacht B by sailing directly up-wind (astern) of B. As A's wind blanket slows B's speed, A will close on B. Then, as A's bow approaches B's stern, A should change course so as to pass B to windward. A must take care not to foul B with either spinnaker or main boom; A must also be prepared to avoid a sudden luff by B, who has luffing rights in this situation.

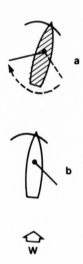

Q.3. How should yacht B attack if yacht A jibes?

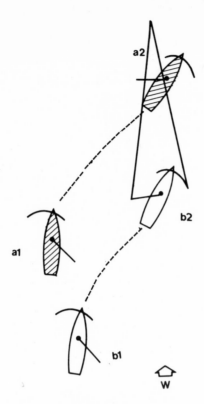

A.3. If yacht A jibes and changes course, yacht B should do the same thing (see illustration). If, however, yacht A jibes and does *not* change course, yacht B may gain by *not* jibing, but by merely maintaining her course so as to continue to blanket yacht A. Remember that each time a yacht jibes, especially in light air, she disturbs the wind flow across her sails and reduces her boat speed slightly. The overriding principle here is to keep the leading yacht in your wind blanket.

Q.4. If you are the leading yacht in the above illustration, how can you best defend yourself against a yacht coming up from astern?

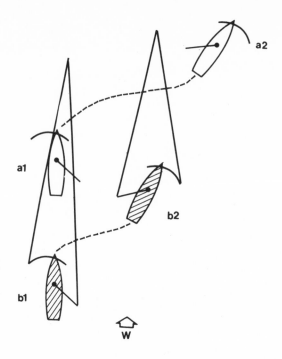

A.4. By changing course to windward, yacht A could gain speed and sail out of yacht B's wind blanket, although, of course, yacht A might no longer be sailing the rhumb line to the next mark. However, yacht A also has the option of jibing and sailing out of yacht B's wind blanket, as illustrated. If B also jibes, A may have to sail even higher, or perhaps jibe again and sail away from B in order to keep her wind clear. This maneuver may have to be repeated a number of times. Take care, however, that a third competitor, sailing a straight line course to the next mark, does not pass or gain significantly while yachts A and B are dueling.

As you can see from comparing the answers to questions 3 and 4, the yacht astern, or behind, becomes the attacking yacht and determines to a great extent the tactics the leading yacht must employ—and the course she must sail—in her efforts to keep her wind clear.

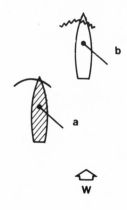

Q.5. What should yacht B do if she finds herself partially blanketed by yacht A, and if her speed has been reduced sufficiently that she cannot luff up past yacht A into clear air?

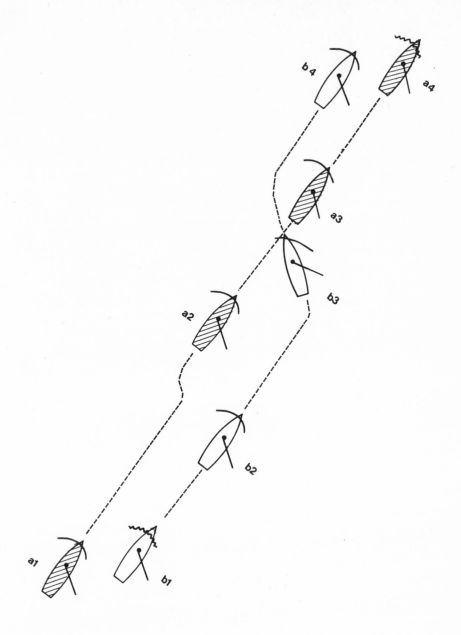

A.5. Yacht B should "turn the tables" on yacht A, let yacht A pass, then sail across her stern and blanket A from behind.

Germany's G 13 leads this group of 5.5-meter yachts in a world's championship race. Note how each trailing yacht is attempting to blanket the competitor ahead. (Photo: Jack Knight)

BELOW AND OPPOSITE PAGE: Classic example of a spinnaker out of control in a hard breeze is International Tempest 117 during the 1972 Olympic Trials. (Photo: Bob Lindgren)

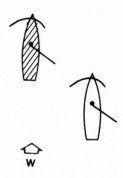

Q.6. Under what conditions should a trailing yacht attempt to pass her competitor to leeward?

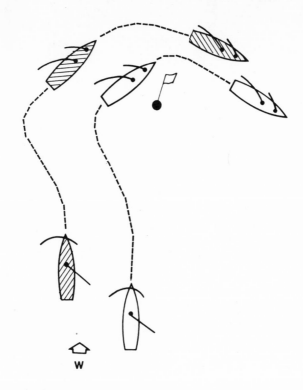

W

A.6. Generally, passing to leeward (on the same side as your competitor's boom) is the safer maneuver, since a yacht being passed to leeward must not bear off below its proper course to prevent you from passing (Rule 39, "Sailing Below a Proper Course").

If you elect to pass to windward, you run the risk of being luffed, in which case a third competitor might pass both of you.

Of great importance in making your decision will be (a) the location of other yachts (will they blanket you as you attempt to pass on one side or the other?), and (b) the distance to the next turning mark, and the side on which that mark is to be left (see illustration). It is most important that you secure an inside overlap at the turning mark, as discussed elsewhere ("Rules" and "Rounding Marks").

Note: Coming up to a leeward turning mark, it is usually more important to secure an inside overlap than to attempt to pass a competitor. When the next leg is to windward, an in-

side position at the mark will put a competitor either in your wind blanket or in your backwind, or it will force him to tack. And remember that the same tactics will work for your competitor if you pass him early in the leg and can't work out far enough ahead of him to be free of his wind blanket. *He* may in turn blanket *you* and secure his own inside overlap before the two-boat-length line is reached.

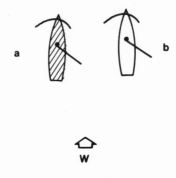

Q.7. How can yacht B get to the other side of yacht A? Is it possible in any way for B to cross A's bow?

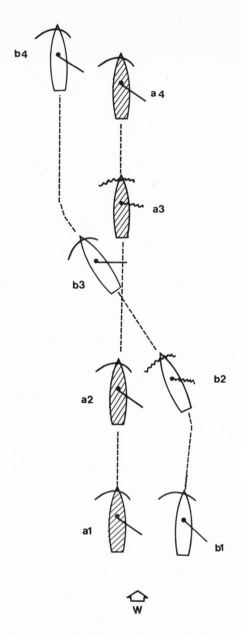

b4

a4

a3

b3

a2

b2

a1

b1

W

A.7. There is no practical way for yacht B to cross yacht A's bow; B must therefore be satisfied with crossing A's stern. If she performs this maneuver properly, however, B should not lose much distance to A, and may even gain on A as a result of temporarily blanketing her. There are several ways that this maneuver can be performed.

Note that at present yacht B is not blanketing yacht A, and is in a slight overlap position. To cross A's stern without hitting A, yacht B will have to bear away from A, then turn to cross astern of her. If B wishes to cross A's stern slowly, in order to blanket A as she goes, B may have to luff slightly (see illustration, position B2) in order to clear A's stern. B would then complete the maneuver described in answer 2, this chapter, blanketing A as she goes.

However, if B wants to get to the other side of A in order to sail away from A on a broad reach (as in a downwind tacking maneuver), she would be better advised to sail further away from A initially, then change course, jibe, and cross A's stern at a sharper angle and increased speed. In this version of the maneuver, B would actually be reaching past A's stern, and would make no attempt to blanket A. Furthermore, B would not have to luff at all as she sailed further away from A in the initial stages of the maneuver.

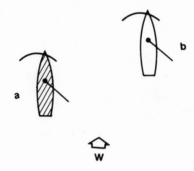

Q.8. In the illustrated position could yacht B cross in front of yacht A?

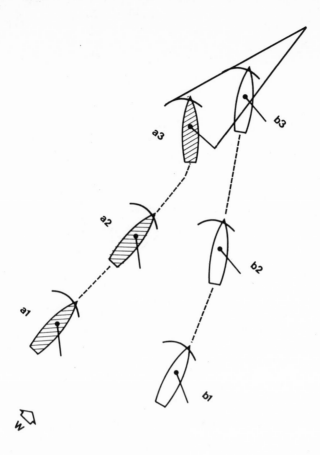

A.8. No, yacht B will not be able to cross in front of yacht A without causing A to change course, since B is only one-half boat length ahead in the illustration. If yacht B were two, or preferably three boat lengths ahead, she would have relatively little difficulty in crossing A's bow, and would minimize the effect of A's wind shadow.

Assuming that yacht B has luffing rights (Rule 38.1), and that she luffs A as shown in the illustration, B has nevertheless placed herself in a very unenviable position. For as she attempts to cross in front of yacht A, yacht B falls into A's wind blanket; if she then continues to try to get clear to windward of A, or even if she attempts to turn back to her original course to get free air, the chances are A will follow her. As illustrated here, it will be nearly impossible for B to break through to the other side (or to windward) of A.

7

Rounding Marks and Finishing

Three Hobie Cats and an Interlake round a leeward mark during the Desert Regatta on Lake Havasu, Arizona. These multi-hull yachts are often not as maneuverable as single-hull yachts. 75 has evidently decided to attempt to break through 8's lee, since she appears to be traveling faster (Rule 37.2). (Note wakes of both yachts.) (Photo: Monk Farnham)

Rounding a leeward mark during the 1972 Olympic Trials, the crew of Tempest US 214 inadvertently touched the mark (Picture 2, BOTTOM OPPOSITE). 214 must now re-round the mark, sacrificing her lead to US 46. (Photo: Bob Lindgren)

Q.1. In this situation, the mark was to have been left to port; but, as the illustration shows, the mark was left to starboard. At position A, the skipper realizes his mistake. How must he properly round to correct his error?

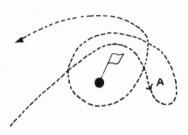

A.1. The skipper must first "unwind" (i.e., sail back along his improper course) before he can begin to round the mark in the proper manner. Imagine that your route through the water is a piece of string; after you have completed all of your maneuvers and the piece of string is pulled taut, it must round the mark on the proper side (see Rule 51.2).

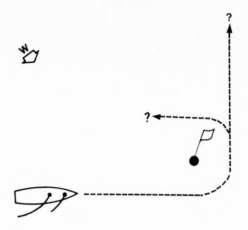

Q.2. After rounding, the course to the next mark is directly to windward. Which of the two courses shown would be the most logical one to take initially after rounding the mark?

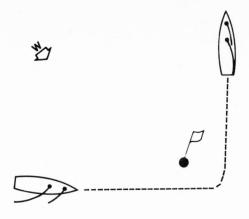

A.2. Assuming there are no yachts directly ahead of you or directly behind you, your best option is to continue on the same tack you were on before rounding. In other words, merely harden up and sail to windward on port tack. If you were to tack onto starboard, as illustrated in the question, you would lose additional momentum as a result of the tacking procedure. (Of course, if there are yachts ahead of you on one tack or the other which could blanket or backwind you, this should influence your decision.)

a

b

Q.3. Should yacht B, in the lead, tack after rounding the mark, or should she remain on the same tack? (Assume that the distance between the two yachts is approximately three boat lengths).

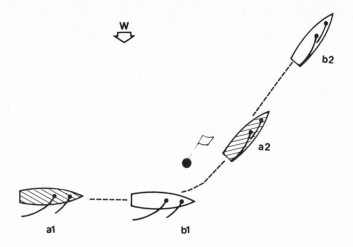

A.3. As long as her opponent does not tack, yacht B should remain on the same tack in order to profit from the "takeoff effect" she gets by trimming her sheets upon rounding. Yacht B should keep an eye on her opponent, however, and be prepared to tack to cover as soon as her opponent does.

a

b

Q.4. How can yacht B maneuver after rounding the mark to be sure of covering yacht A, regardless of A's tactics?

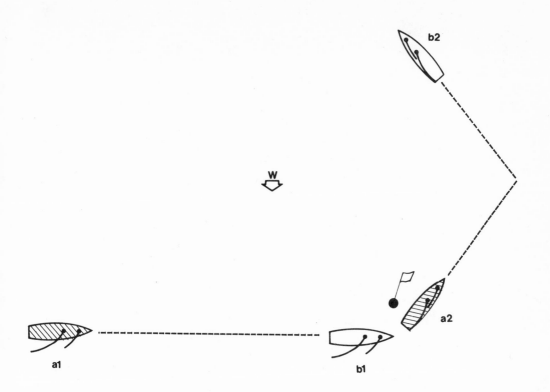

A.4. Yacht A will probably "split tacks" with yacht B. In other words, yacht A will observe the tack yacht B chooses after rounding the mark, and will in most cases take the other tack after she herself rounds. In this way, yacht A will not be covered and will have free air.

Yacht B can employ one tactic, however, that will ensure her of being directly to windward of yacht A no matter which tack A selects after rounding: a tactic very often used in match racing. Before rounding, yacht B estimates the distance between herself and yacht A. After hardening up on port tack upon rounding, yacht B sails half the estimated distance between the two yachts on port tack, and the other half on starboard tack. B will thus be directly to windward of yacht A as A rounds the mark, as shown in the illustration. If yacht A tacks onto starboard, yacht B will have yacht A in her wind shadow. Or, if there is significant distance (more than five

boat lengths) between the two, yacht B will at least be directly to windward of yacht A.

If yacht A elects to continue on port tack, however, yacht B should tack onto port in order to keep A covered. In either case B is directly to windward of yacht A and should be in a controlling situation.

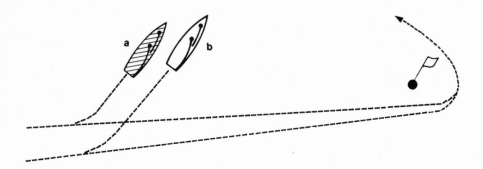

Q.5. In the illustration, yacht B has luffing rights over yacht A. Should she continue to luff A above her course to the next mark?

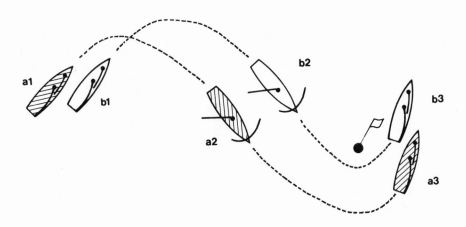

A.5. Yacht B's tactics in this situation will depend on how close astern other yachts might be. If this is a two-boat race, or if there are no other competitors close astern, B should continue to sail high of the course, luffing A, until B's backwind and wave action cause A to fall astern. Yacht A, at this point, will probably turn for the mark. Yacht B should follow suit as this will leave her on the inside position coming into the mark.

It is important that B maintain her inside overlap at the two-boat-length position. If yacht A should blanket her and pull clear ahead, yacht B should in turn blanket A, slow her down, and attempt to reestablish her inside overlap before reaching the two-boat-length position.

If B cannot get A to turn toward the mark first, then B will eventually *have* to turn, but she should attempt to keep her wind clear and maintain her inside position at the mark.

If there are other competitors close astern, B may have to turn toward the mark earlier and take the chance of being passed by A in order to maintain her lead over the yachts coming up astern.

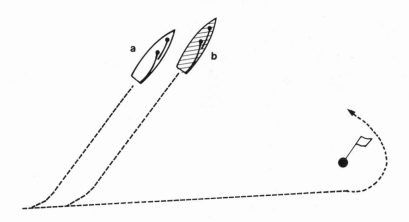

Q.6. How can yacht A maneuver in this situation to gain an advantage over yacht B?

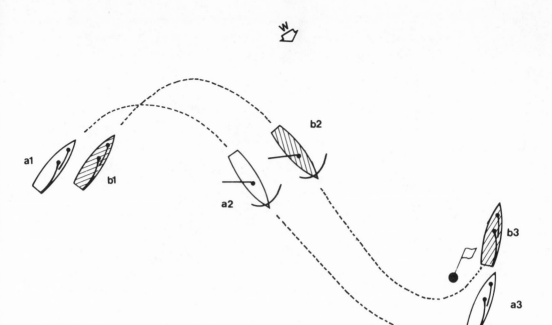

A.6. It will be most difficult for yacht A to gain an inside over-lap at this turning mark, since A is being luffed by yacht B, who has right-of-way, and A does not know how long B will continue this tactic. Yacht A's only recourse is to ease sheets, fall clear astern of B, and turn for the mark.

If A can manage to get to the two-boat-length line clear ahead of B, A will round ahead of B. To discourage this, and in order to establish her own inside overlap, yacht B will probably try to blanket A. Yacht A should consider sailing high of the mark in order to keep her wind free.

In summary: it will be very difficult for yacht A to break clear ahead of B and establish for herself an inside overlap at the mark.

Snipes round a mark overlapped during the Wolverine Regatta in
Ann Arbor, Michigan. 511 has an overlap on 8046 who in turn has
one on 14323. Outside boat must sail wide enough of the mark to give
adequate room to all competitors with inside overlaps (Rule 42.1).
There appears to have been a foul or a collision between 11147 and
16743, given their current situation. (Photo: Fred Butler)

Tempest 162 has sailed high of her course to the leeward mark to keep
any of her competitors from getting an inside overlap (Photo 1,
BELOW). But she now must initially swing wide in order to round close
to the mark and prevent 277 from shooting up to windward of her
after the rounding (Photos 2 and 3, OPPOSITE). (Photo: Bob Lindgren)

Q.7. In this three-boat situation, how should the leading yacht steer in order to protect her position?

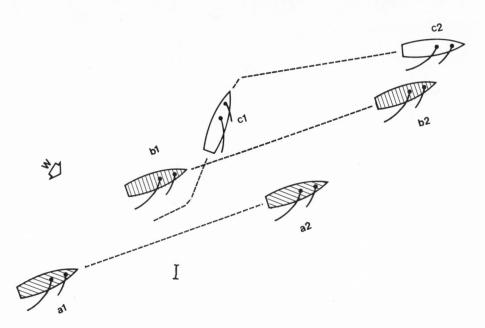

I

A.7. Yacht C should try, as quickly as possible, to discourage yacht B from attempting to pass to windward, so that she can bear off for the mark and protect against yacht A. To do this, yacht C might luff quite decisively in order to (1) discourage yacht B from attempting to pass to windward, and (2) prompt B to bear off directly for the mark (illustration 1).

If this tactic is not successful, yacht C might bear off suddenly and drive for the mark herself, hoping that yacht B does not blanket her, and establish an inside overlap before the two-boat-length position is reached. See illustration 2.

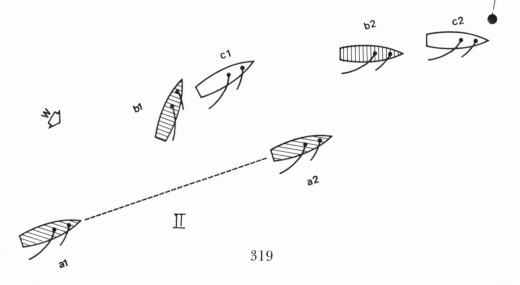

II

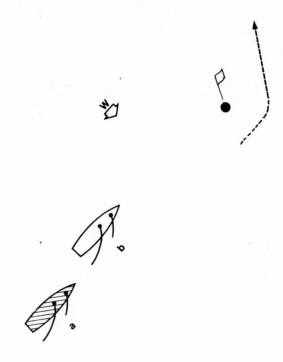

Q.8. How can yacht B protect herself?

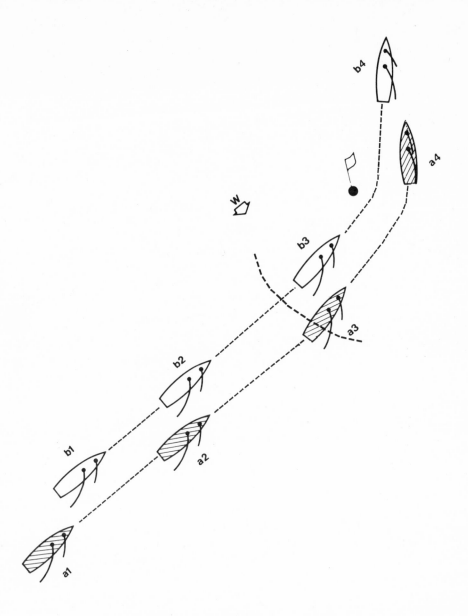

A.8. To make certain she will have a legal inside overlap at the mark, yacht B may wish to slow down sufficiently to lure yacht A into an outside overlap. If this tactic is successful, yacht B will have prevented A from crossing her stern and riding up to an inside overlap position at the two-boat-length line. In effect, yacht B, in position B2, by slowing down, locks A out of any chance at an inside position.

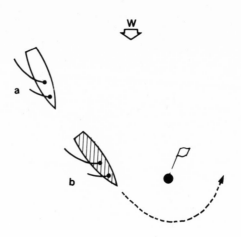

Q.9. How might yacht A attempt to break free of yacht B's covering tactics after they round the mark?

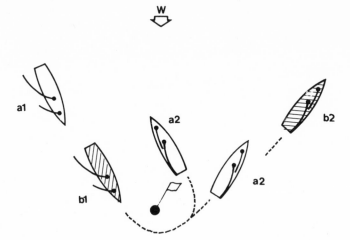

A.9. Yacht A can, if she wishes, attempt to bear off and drive through yacht B's wind shadow after rounding. However, A is already clear astern of B, and will lose momentum as she rounds. Two better choices are illustrated (positions A2 and B2).

Yacht A can either remain on port tack, point higher, and attempt to work herself to windward out of yacht B's back-wind, which tactic will slow her down; or she can tack immediately after rounding. This latter tactic will cost yacht A distance, since she will have tacked before gaining full speed after rounding. On the other hand, by tacking immediately after rounding, she will be sailing in clear air.

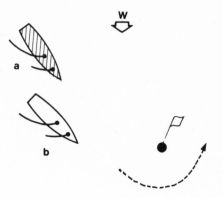

Q.10. Assuming that the yachts were overlapped when the leading yacht reached the two-boat-length line, what should yacht B do?

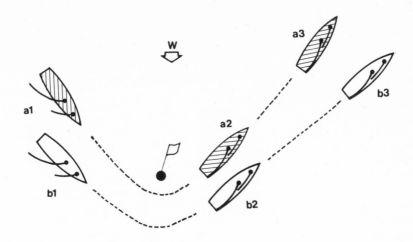

A.10. Because yacht B has no rights in rounding this mark, she must keep clear of yacht A, and will thus end up sailing a longer course than A. Yacht B can minimize this disadvantage, however, by rounding as close to yacht A as possible, so as not to sail a *significantly* greater distance than yacht A. After rounding, B should bear off slightly, gain speed, and attempt to sail out from under yacht A's wind blanket. In position B3, yacht B has accomplished this. Yacht B might now sail hard on the wind on the same course as yacht A and attempt to establish a safe leeward position.

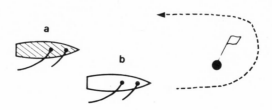

Q.11. Yachts A and B were overlapped when yacht B reached the two-boat-length line. The overlap has now been broken. The course to the next mark is either a beat or close reach on starboard tack. What is yacht B's proper tactic?

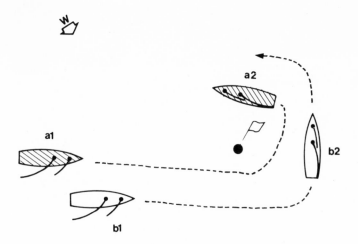

A.11. Despite the fact that the overlap has been broken, yacht A retains her rights over yacht B (Rules 42.1(a)(i) and 42.2(c)(i). Yacht A will probably round the mark and immediately tack onto starboard. However, her speed will be substantially slowed by these two maneuvers occurring close together.

Yacht B would be wise to round and remain on port tack (keeping clear of A in doing so), sail on port tack until she is two or three boat lengths to windward of yacht A's course, and then tack onto starboard. In this position, yacht B will be sailing in clear air and will be far enough to windward to be unaffected by yacht A's backwind. If this short port tack causes her to overstand the next mark, her loss will still be less than if she attempted to sail in yacht A's backwind for the entire leg.

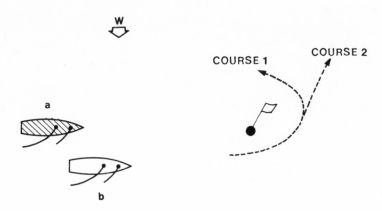

Q.12. Much has been said in this book about the importance of the inside position at a turning mark. The inside yacht obviously travels a shorter distance, has complete control over the rounding maneuver, and sails in clear air if the next leg is to windward.

In the illustration above, the next turning mark is *not* directly to windward, but is *either* in the direction of course arrow 1 or of course arrow 2. (The course will either be a beat on port tack, or a close reach on starboard.)

Therefore, will yacht B lose the same amount of distance to yacht A during the rounding process, regardless of the direction of the next leg?

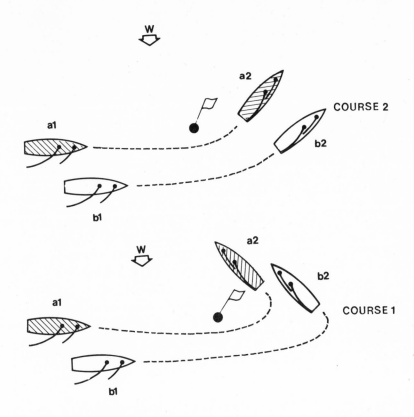

A.12. No, because, in general, the greater the turning angle at a mark, the more the outside yacht suffers. Thus, in the illustrations shown, course 1 has caused yacht B to fall further behind, and has placed her in a more difficult position.

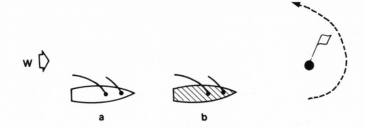

Q.13. Is there a possibility that yacht A can gain on yacht B?

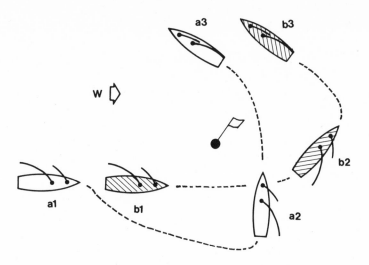

A.13. Only if yacht B rounds the mark poorly! Yacht A has
not established an inside overlap, and must keep clear of
yacht B during the rounding maneuver. In the diagram, yacht
B has rounded the mark wide and inadvertently left room inside
for yacht A. Given this opportunity, yacht A's tactic is to
sail wide initially going into the turn, then jibe and round
up sharply inside and to weather of yacht B. Although yacht
A does not have rights in this situation, and is therefore gam-
bling, her maneuver can often be very effective. It all depends
upon an alert skipper perceiving a leading yacht initiating her
turn too close to the mark, thus inevitably rounding wide.

5.5-meter yacht US 31 has rounded the leeward mark inside S 40 and is "pinching" or pointing very high to work out of S 40's backwind. (Photo: Frederic Maura, Bahamas News Bureau)

Tempests at the leeward mark during the 1972 Olympic Trials. 233 has rounded and tacked to starboard. She may elect to sail one half the distance of her estimated lead over 270 and then tack back onto port. If she then tacks each time 270 tacks, she will cover 270 very effectively. (Photo: Bob Lindgren)

Approaching the finish line during the 1972 Olympics, Dragon G 037 on starboard tack has right of way; her port-tack competitors must either tack or bear off (Rule 36). The telephoto lens used makes the yachts appear to be closer to a collision than they are. (Photo: K. Hashimoto)

International Star Class yacht 4820 "rolls over" a competitor to take third place during the 1971 World Championship. (Photo: Roy Montgomery)

Q.14. Should yacht A try to pass yacht B to windward or to leeward? (Yacht B is about six boat lengths from the turning mark.)

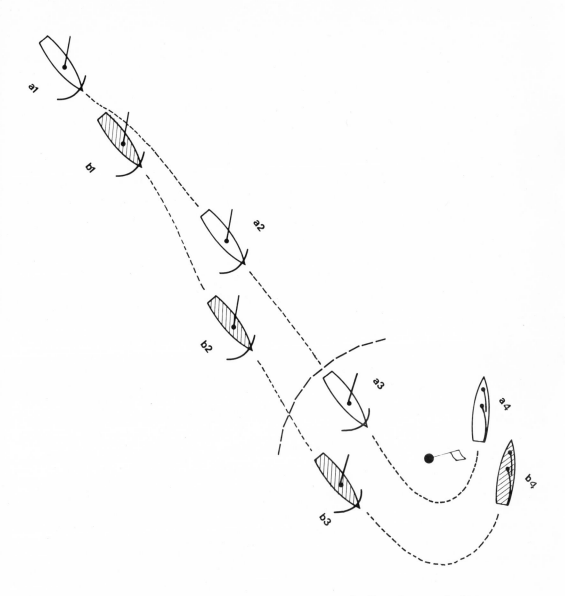

A.14. Yacht A should attempt to pass yacht B to leeward, first by blanketing yacht B, and second by establishing an overlap to leeward . . . which becomes an inside overlap when the two-boat-length position is reached. Obviously, yacht A, having the inside overlap at the mark, will come out in the commanding position after the turn.

Q.15. Should yacht A continue on this course when the turning mark is to be left to port?

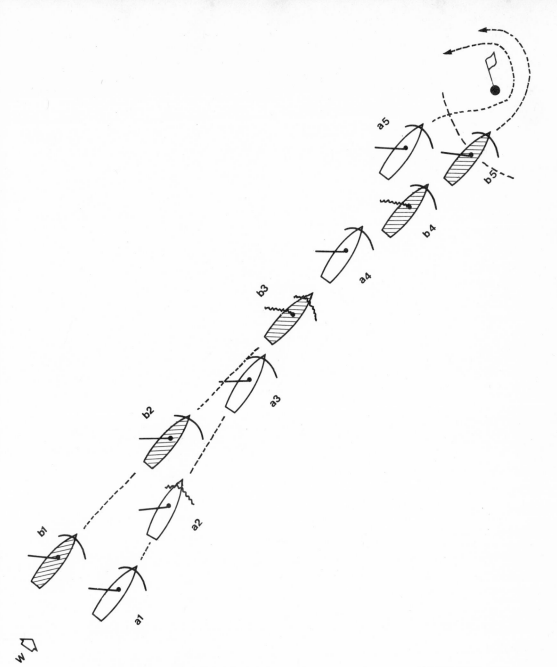

A.15. No. Yacht A should attempt to slow down enough to cross yacht B's stern and secure an inside overlap at the two-boat-length position. Yacht A, in position A2, has slowed by collapsing her spinnaker momentarily, and in position 3 is in turn slowing yacht B by blanketing her. At position 4 yacht A has established her inside overlap.

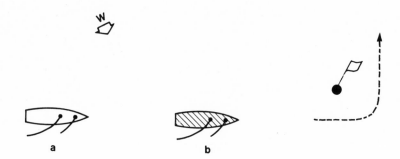

Q.16. If yacht A is approximately two boat lengths behind yacht B before rounding the mark, how should yacht A maneuver *after* rounding to best sail in clear air?

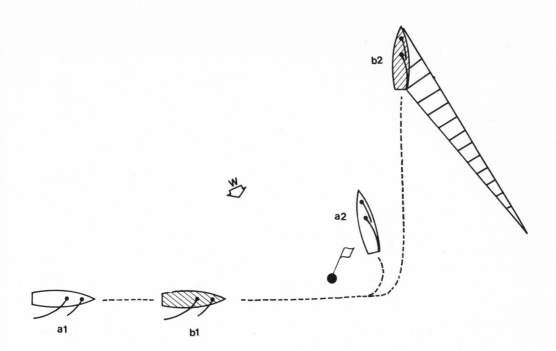

A.16. Since yacht A is two boat lengths behind yacht B, the effect of yacht B's backwind will be diminished. Yacht A, as shown in position A2, might attempt to sail a little higher than yacht B in order to place herself even further from yacht B's backwind. If she is still affected, she might consider tacking to gain clear air.

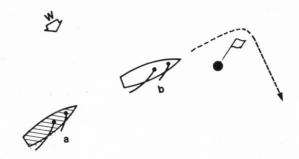

Q.17. What course should yacht B steer after rounding the mark?

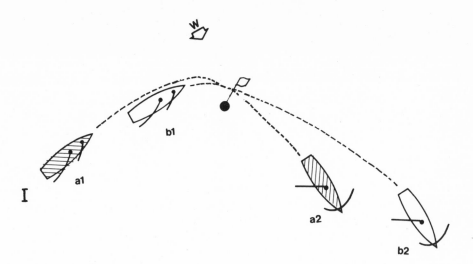

A.17. As shown in illustration 1, yacht B should sail slightly high of a rhumb-line course after rounding, so that yacht A will not be tempted to blanket her. Illustration 2 shows what might happen if yacht B merely sailed directly for the next mark after rounding.

Yacht B must continue to maneuver so as to keep her wind clear, and must therefore watch her opponent closely.

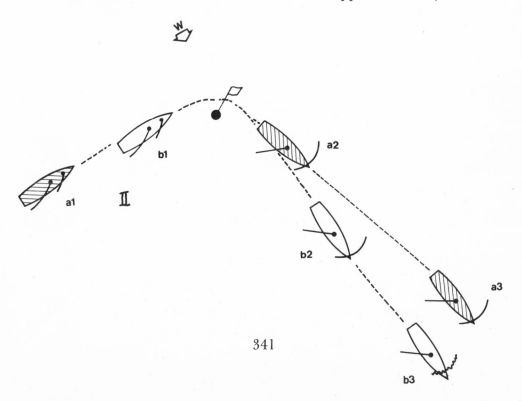

341

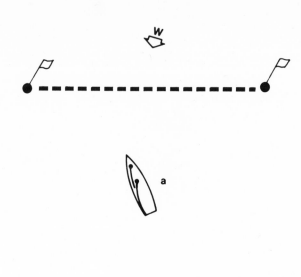

Q.18. Assuming both yachts are still five or more boat lengths from the finish line and the wind has been shifting, what should yacht A do?

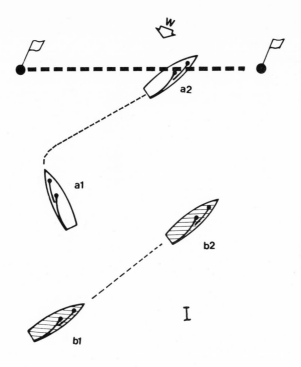

A.18. In most cases, especially if the wind has been shifting, yacht A should immediately tack and cover yacht B to the finish line, as in illustration 1.

Illustration 2 shows what might happen if yacht A did not tack to cover and the wind were to back (shift in a counter-

clockwise direction). Yacht A would then be headed, and would not be able to lay the finish line on starboard tack. Yacht B, on the other hand, might receive enough of a lift to now lay the finish line without tacking. Yacht A's lead has been cut considerably. This illustrates the danger of not closely covering a following yacht under shifting wind conditions.

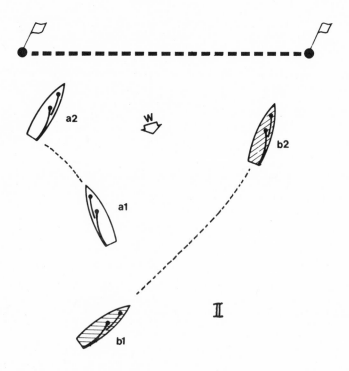

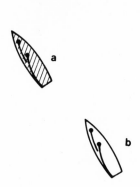

Q.19. How should yacht B approach the finish line?

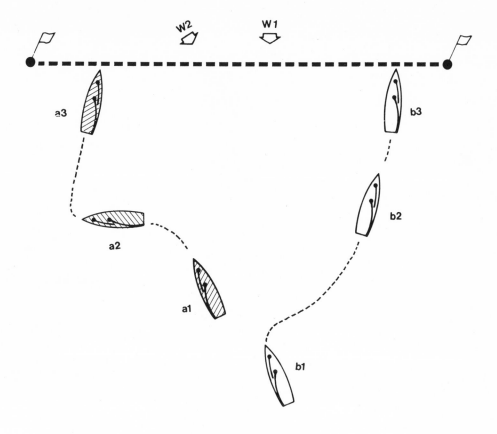

A.19. Yacht B should immediately tack onto port. If yacht A tacks to cover, the yachts will probably next meet on the starboard tack layline to the finish, with yacht B on starboard tack. Although she will not *necessarily* gain by this maneuver, yacht B has nothing to lose by attempting it. She will also be sailing in clear air.

If yacht B tacks onto port and yacht A does *not* tack to cover, and if the wind backs (from W1 to W2), yacht B will be lifted to the finish line and will be able to cross without tacking, whereas yacht A will no longer be able to lay the line and will have to tack onto port to do so. In this situation, yacht B has caught yacht A, and might beat her across the finish line.